Praise for *Get Your Own Coffee* and Suzanne Hopgood

Reading *Get Your Own Coffee* is like sitting down for lunch with a friend, attending class with your favorite teacher, and having coffee with a wise mentor—all in one experience.

In each story Suzanne shares, there are powerful lessons in principled leadership, navigating a male-dominated culture, taking bold professional and personal risks, and turning adversity into opportunity.

No matter where you are in your own professional or personal journey, Suzanne's life stories offer invaluable insights, presented with her signature blend of directness, candor, and humor.

Thank you, Suzanne, for sharing so much of your remarkable life so we can all learn from it.

—Bonnie Malley

Vice President, Finance and Administration

Chief Financial Officer, Hartford Foundation for Public Giving

Suzanne's experiences in life and business as related in *Get Your Own Coffee* are interesting, instructive, and entertaining. She provides example after example of how her upbringing, attitudes, values, personal strategies, and dedicated relationship-building contributed to overcoming even the most outrageous prejudices, setbacks, and forces of opposition to produce great personal and business satisfaction and success. Among the keys: finding and sharing the humor in almost any situation and a huge heart and empathy for people from every walk of life.

Beginning in the late 1990s, a time when women serving on public company boards were few, Suzanne was a leader in the post-Enron revolution in public company governance, serving on six male-dominated public company boards. Even more impressively, she overcame initial skepticism and discomfort to be elected board chair of three of them. Called upon by some of the largest institutional investors in the US to advocate for improved governance at companies like Disney and J.P. Morgan, she was an invited speaker on corporate governance at more than one hundred public companies, private companies, and business and governance organizations. Anyone working in or seeking to penetrate the highest levels of corporate and civic leadership and responsibility will find valuable tips and lessons in her book.

—Michael W. Tankersley

Senior Counsel, Alston & Bird

Founding Director, Texas Business Law Foundation

get your own coffee

Suzanne Hopgood

get your own coffee

Underestimated, Overlooked, and Now The Boss

Advantage | Books

Published by Advantage Books, Charleston, South Carolina.
An imprint of Advantage Media.

Printed in the United States of America.

10 9 8 7 6 5 4 3 2 1

ISBN: 979-8-89188-095-5 (Paperback)
ISBN: 979-8-89188-096-2 (eBook)

Library of Congress Control Number: 2025913248

Cover design by Analisa Smith.
Layout design by Ruthie Wood.

07-25-2025 8:57

To Frank C. Lord, my best friend and companion for forty years and the love of my life.

Contents

Acknowledgments

When I finished writing this book, I sat back and thought, *I have had a truly wonderful life.* I would like to acknowledge a few of the wonderful people who made that possible.

Bonnie Malley, for convincing me that sharing my story would help others.

Mike Tankersley, for always being there to help with the tough decisions.

Team Frank: Dr. Bob, Kathy Tummillo, Leroy Samuels, Dwayne Greenland, Tracey, and Steve Lamantini.

Fr. Curtis and Rev. Charlie, for helping me grieve and for blessing Frank's ashes.

Junette Pearson, my best friend since kindergarten (seventy years!).

Glenda Reed, Nancy Lease, and Barbara Durepo, who helped me through corporate Aetna.

Bill Russell, who mentored and encouraged me.

Rachel Roginsky, who stepped up and allowed me to become chair/CEO of Furr's.

Connecticut Supreme Court Justice Andrew McDonald, for recommending me as the Capital Region Development Authority (CRDA) chair.

Mike Freimuth, the best real estate guy I've ever met and the best executive director, who made CRDA rewarding and fun.

David Robinson, chair of CRDA and retired general counsel of The Hartford.

Chion Wolf, for her amazing perspective on the world.

Introduction

Dear Reader,

The seed for writing this book was planted by my good friend Bonnie Malley. "Suzanne," she said, "There are so many leaders who are motivated by ego and accolades. People don't need to hear about more of them. People need to hear about the leaders who are motivated by getting things done right for the people they work with, their community, and their family and friends. You are that leader."

I hadn't really considered what type of leader I was until Bonnie shared that piece of wisdom with me. She was right. I will work incredibly hard to get the best possible outcome for my family, friends, clients, and community, and I choose to do so with as little recognition as possible. It wasn't until I was writing the conclusion for this book that I realized my leadership style was no accident. You will soon hear what an incredible role model my mother was for me, and you will see her incredible list of accomplishments—a list that was unknown to me until after my mother's passing, when members of the Littleton Garden Club helped put her obituary together. My parents were not people who sought accolades for their accomplishments; they simply worked hard to do what they believed was right. Both of my parents modeled the non-ego-driven leadership style—a style that, as Bonnie wisely pointed out, is not as common as it should be.

In the '80s, '90s, and early 2000s, I was often the only woman, or one of the few women, at the higher echelons of corporate leadership. As such, I had to navigate many leaders who chose to feed their own egos rather than do what was best for the company and its employees, customers, and community. In between those leaders, however, I have been lucky enough to meet others who chose to lead by lifting their people up. The best thing I ever did for my career was to listen to those leaders who believed in me.

When the head of the department in the savings bank I worked at recommended I apply for a job with another bank as the department head in charge of lending—I listened.

When the department head of a $33 billion real estate investment division of a Fortune 500 company (and my boss's boss) continually and intentionally expanded my knowledge, experience, contacts, and opportunities, I listened to the message of how capable he believed me to be, and I began to believe it, too, and acted on his advice.

When the largest investment companies and an Ivy League school hired me as a consultant, I listened to their trust in me. When shareholders voted me in as chair and CEO of a New York Stock Exchange (NYSE) company despite my lack of public company experience or experience managing a company with five thousand employees, I listened to their confidence in my ability to get the job done.

I have also always listened to the smartest (and most humble) person I've ever known—my husband, Frank Lord, who always had confidence in me and pushed me to do more than I thought I could.

Seek out the leaders who believe in you and support you. Listen to their message and then go be that kind of leader.

Chapter 1

Where the Story Ends

As I stepped into the lobby and surveyed the crowd attending the 2021 annual Hartford Public Library gala, I turned to make my first wisecrack of the evening to Frank, but the words caught in my throat. Resisting the urge to reach out and touch him, I braced myself for the hundred-foot wave of grief that engulfed me.

This was the first fundraising event I had attended since the COVID-19 lockdowns. My husband, Frank, and I had been frequent flyers at these types of events—Frank more often than me, as, in his retirement, he had fully immersed himself in volunteering in our community of Hartford, Connecticut, while I was still traveling for my work.

Tonight, there would be none of our usual playful bantering. There would also be no "What do you think?"—the signal we would give each other when one of us was ready to go but was also fine with staying longer if the other one wasn't ready just yet.

Standing there alone, my eyes wandering the room, it hit me that I didn't know what to do. I had always thought of myself as the socialite of the two of us, but the truth I now understood was that it had been Frank whom everyone had known, and it was Frank who had moved through these rooms with ease. I had simply followed his lead and joined in. I had known tonight—one of many firsts without Frank by my side—would be tough, but I was not prepared for the waves of grief that threatened to wash me away.

I searched the faces in the crowd for my friend, Bonnie, who had agreed to be my anchor that evening. When I found her, she effortlessly enveloped me in whatever conversation she was having. And that is how the rest of the evening went. I would venture off on my own for a bit, and when I felt the waters rising again, I would return to Bonnie for a steadying hand.

Frank, my husband of thirty-seven years, had died a little more than a year earlier, on July 3, 2020. Frank was six feet four to my five feet two. He was a trickster, an actuary at The Hartford, a voracious reader, an outdoorsman, an avid consumer of performing arts, and he was the kindest man I have ever met. He had also been my best friend and loving companion for almost forty years.

During that first year after Frank's death, I had allowed myself to remain secluded in the lockdown bubble except for walking the riverfront every morning with my friend Jennifer. The lockdown provided me with the opportunity to grieve in peace and the time to begin putting together the pieces of what would become my life's next chapter without Frank by my side (a chapter, I decided that night, that would no longer include attending galas).

It was a struggle to imagine my future without Frank. He had been through every big and small moment with me for almost forty years. He had been my rock when I was fired from Aetna; my companion and personal GPS (we could be in the middle of a subway station in a foreign country, and Frank would magically know exactly where we were and where we needed to go—left to my own devices, I would still be in said subway) when I traveled on business to Rio, São Paulo, Moscow,

Beijing, and Hong Kong; and the planner extraordinaire of our annual trips spent bicycling through Europe, Canada, and Southeast Asia.

Frank saw me as his intellectual equal in an age when women in an office were only allowed, encouraged, and believed capable of getting coffee and typing up the important words that only men delivered. Over the years, there were many times in my career when I felt unmoored—not related to my ability to get the job done but because of the toxic environments I worked in. Environments where I was so often underestimated, undermined, and unsupported by my male counterparts. In every instance, Frank had been my trusted sounding board, champion of all I was capable of, and a source of laughter even in the most trying of times.

I have almost always been the only woman at the senior leadership table, but I still managed to experience tremendous success, in part because of who I am, in part because of my parents and the environment they raised me in, in part because of the incredible mentors and friends I was fortunate to find along the way, and in part because of my long and loving partnership with Frank.

And so, I begin with Frank, because my story cannot be told without understanding the pivotal role he played in my ability to have such a successful career and live such an amazing and full life.

I first met Frank at a party my friend Sylvia and I decided to host when we realized there were single men in our condo building whom we did not know.

"What are we going to do about that?" she asked me.

"We need to throw a party," I suggested.

And that's just what we did. Frank arrived at the party, apologizing in the same breath as introducing himself, explaining that he would need to leave early because he had tickets to a chamber concert later that evening.

Hmm, I thought. *Maybe this is what my shrink meant when she said I needed to expand the type of people I was associating with*—which, at the time, had been primarily single-focused, highly driven real estate men who were definitely not attending chamber concerts. I had been seeing said therapist since leaving my first husband after he had assaulted me—after which I did not call the police or press charges. In 1976, a husband assaulting his wife was considered a "domestic disturbance," not a criminal activity, and the prevailing wisdom had been that such "disturbances" were best worked out by the parties involved—the one committing the assault and the one being assaulted.

So, meeting a well-mannered and cultured man like Frank seemed like the right opportunity to expand my horizons, and boy, was it ever. I would quickly realize that, unlike so many men at that time, Frank not only believed in my ability (and the abilities of women) to succeed in business (or anything else they set out to do), but he also did everything he could to support my efforts, and I his.

A couple of years after we were married, I was very sick. My doctor told me that people my age (mid-thirties at the time) who chose to subject themselves to high-stress, sixty-to-seventy-hour workweeks would come to her expecting her to prescribe a pill that would allow them to return to a grueling work schedule rather than take the time to allow their mind and body to recover and heal. "I'm not that person," she told me, "So, you've got one of two choices, Suzanne. You go on vacation, or I put you in the hospital." I agreed to go on vacation.

"And after that vacation," my doctor further instructed, "you need to get away and completely disconnect from the daily grind of constant pressure, at least once a quarter if you want to remain healthy." She knew I would work all day, every day, until I dropped.

Frank took the doctor's instructions very seriously, but never once did he suggest I stop working. Instead, he took charge of arranging quarterly getaways and annual international trips for us. Without fail, I would protest that I didn't have time to go away, and without fail, Frank would ignore my protests, request my schedule, and then plan accordingly. It would be years before I stopped being surprised that the world didn't end every time I disconnected from work—and back then, it was a true disconnect. There were no cell phones and certainly no Wi-Fi. When you were away from work, you were truly away.

Yes, people could reach you on a landline—but you had to actually be near the landline to receive the call, and Frank and I were definitely not sitting by the phone when we went away. On weekends, we retreated to Old Saybrook, Connecticut. First as day trips (as it was just forty-five minutes from Hartford) and later to the vacation home we eventually purchased at the shore. Those weekends included a daily bike trip to breakfast, during which we would decide which route we would cycle that day. Forty or fifty miles later and on our way back, we'd stop at the fish or meat market so Frank could purchase dinner ingredients and then ride home with panniers full of whatever he needed to make our dinner that evening. We didn't socialize a lot on weekends; instead, we biked and read.

When my department head, who would go on to become my mentor, signed me up for the all-guy golf tournament, knowing I didn't play, Frank and I learned—together. Both our fathers had taught us the basics of golf when we were younger, but neither of us was particularly good at it. I began taking lessons once a week, sharing what I learned with Frank. Early on in my lessons, my instructor said, "You're not going to learn how to play golf just with me. You're going to learn at the driving range and the putting green. Just keep at it." So, in the months leading up to the tournament, Frank and I would spend time every weekend on the golf course in Old Saybrook and every weeknight at the driving range near our home in Hartford to make sure I was ready (and I was, but more on that later).

Frank and I were partners in every sense of the word. We loved each other, supported each other, and truly enjoyed being with each other. We discussed and shared everything. Some of our discussions resulted in developing scripts to help us through difficult situations. I can vividly recall creating our first script. I had been highly offended at a board meeting when an Amarillo, Texas, banker sitting beside me had made a racist comment. I was speechless. I went home that night and said to Frank, "I need a script."

I knew that if I said nothing in these situations, it would seem as if I agreed with the person's opinion, but I also didn't think it appropriate for me to jump up on my soapbox. Frank and I talked through the situation and came up with the following script—one we've both used a hundred times over the years—"I'm offended by what you just said. I think if we just attend to business, it would be better for all of us."

Another script we created was prompted by one of my clients requesting that I fudge the financial projections I had prepared for them after extensive market research. They'd returned the pro forma projections and told me that I would need to redo them to increase the cash flow forecast. They needed these pro forma forecasts to obtain financing for the hotel they were planning on building. I was well-known and respected in the financial community, so my work would be respected.

I was extremely upset by the request, and that evening, I said to Frank, "My largest client, who owes me a lot of money, is essentially asking me to lie on the financials."

"Well," he said, "you don't really have a choice."

"I know," I said. "But they are my largest client, and they owe me a lot of money. If I don't get that money, we could lose the house."

Frank looked at me and said, "OK, then. We might lose the house."

I, of course, did not fudge the numbers (and we did not, thankfully, lose the house), but I did lose my client and the money owed to me. At the end of that debacle, Frank and I developed another script: "No one is hurt; no one is in the hospital; no one died. It's only money." Our ethics were our gold standard, and we were not willing to forfeit them under any circumstance. This was especially true for Frank, because even if held at gunpoint, Frank couldn't tell a lie, no matter how inconsequential—he just couldn't.

The most important gift Frank and I shared was a sense of humor. Humor was so important to us that, early in our marriage, Frank committed to making sure we started every day with a laugh.

It was almost always over simple things, really. He might say, "Is that a new look?"

"Is what a new look?" I'd ask.

He'd point to my leg and say, "That run in your stocking."

And there was the laugh that would begin our day.

One of my favorite things to say to Frank was, "I love you to the moon and back."

He'd look at me, all serious, and say, "Listen, I'm not going to the moon just to love you."

Even after his stroke, Frank kept his commitment to making me laugh. Once Frank's cognition improved, his old trickster ways returned. One afternoon, he said he wanted an egg salad sandwich for lunch, which I thought was strange since I had never seen him eat an egg salad sandwich. But off I went and picked up some egg salad and made him a sandwich.

He didn't eat it. When I asked him if he was going to eat it, he said, "Well, I really wanted egg salad from Walt's." (Walt's is in Old Saybrook.)

"Really?" I asked. "You want me to drive to Old Saybrook, get egg salad at Walt's, drive back home, make you a sandwich, and then watch you *not* eat it?"

He smiled.

"Yeah," I said, with a grin of my own. "That's not going to happen."

It is only now, as I write this book, that I realize it's Frank's life-sustaining humor I miss the most. That's what hit me so hard at the Hartford Public Library gala in 2021—turning to make that first wisecrack of the evening before remembering he wasn't beside me. That was tough and still is. I have no shortage of intelligent friends whom I can call and talk to about anything, but Frank's and my shared love of easy, playful banter, which we engaged in every single day of our life together, just doesn't work with anyone else.

Two years after losing Frank, I turned my life upside down and returned to my hometown of Littleton, New Hampshire. Staying in Hartford, every place I went, Frank was missing, and I just couldn't live in that bubble of sadness. But I haven't forsaken Hartford. Frank and I had built a life together there, and he had given so much to the Hartford community. It was important to me that I continue to honor his legacy, and that honoring began with Frank's memorial service in Bushnell Park.

Frank loved Bushnell Park, and he loved ice cream. So, two hundred of us gathered in the park for the dedication of what would be the park's new summer music series ice cream cart (complete with Frank's picture on its side). Our priest, Father Curtis, was a willing participant in the shenanigans masquerading as a service, offering both the dedication prayer and the blessing of the ice cream cart. The whole affair was hilarious. I would later go on to sponsor, in Frank's name, a summer music series, virtual author interviews at his beloved Mark Twain House, a scholarship fund for Hartford students to further their schooling, specific performances at the local live theaters, and activities at Hartford Public Library.

Now you know where my story ended (for now), but of course, there is no end without, first, a beginning. My trajectory into the world of boardrooms began when I was two years old. If you don't believe me, just keep reading.

Chapter 2

It All Started in the Kitchen

My mother was beautiful, utterly charming, and precise, with crystal clear expectations: Treat everyone with respect, period. There was no looking down on people or wising off, and back talk was certainly not tolerated. Her simple, "Young lady, we do not behave like that," ended any discussion. This is why, at the age of two, I knew how to comport myself without understanding I was doing so—a skill that has served me well in my career and life. I confess, I have sat in many board and community meetings in which I have been tempted to channel my mother, Rita C. McAvoy, and say, "Young lady/young man, we do not behave like that here," but somehow, I don't think it would have had the same impact as when my mother said it to me.

In the 1950s, society expected women to set marriage as their number one goal. The few women who were encouraged to go to college during that time were encouraged to do so not for their BA but for their "MRS" degree. This would still be the common refrain when I went off to college in the late '60s, along with a limited selection of careers considered appropriate for women while they continued their search for their husband and the wedded bliss that would surely follow. Those career options were teacher, nurse, or secretary.

My mother was none of the above. For the first two years of my life, my parents and I lived in Thayer's Hotel, a business they would own and operate for more than twenty years. In an equal partnership, my parents ran their hotel with efficiency, respect, and rules. My mother set and modeled the rules and expectations for appropriate behavior early on, and I followed them, as did my father and every employee of their hotel.

And so, I remember being baffled when my high school guidance counselor told me, "Women are nurses or teachers, so those are the schools you need to look at." I looked at him like he had three heads—clearly, he couldn't be bothered to understand me at all. If he had, he would have known that science was not in my skill set, and as for teaching, when my parents had begun offering me the option at the age of eleven to either stay home and babysit my four nieces and nephews or bus tables at the hotel, I chose bussing tables (or anything else they wanted me to do) every time, because babysitting toddlers was the definition of hell to me. Even if my guidance counselor hadn't figured out that I did not have a personality that suited nursing or teaching, I sure had. Besides, long before high school, I knew I wanted to run my own business. I saw the lifestyle and the freedom business ownership afforded my father *and* my mother, and I wanted the same.

My hometown of Littleton, New Hampshire, may not have seemed like the place to achieve this aim, but for a small, rural town, Littleton turned out to be an exceptionally worldly place to grow up.

While Littleton might appear to be just a sleepy little town nestled within two river valleys, it has served as a vibrant "crossroads of northern New England" since the nineteenth century. Its population (4,758 in 1950 and 6,036 in 2023[1]) and demographics (primarily White and blue-collar) remain largely unchanged. Initially, Littleton thrived through its mills, tanneries, and factories, with the Connecticut River serving as a gateway for their products.

Once the railway arrived in 1853, Littleton flourished as a transportation hub, with banks, law offices, restaurants, and shops springing up to serve the influx of travelers. Grand hotels, including Thayer's, established Littleton's reputation for hospitality. Even as traditional industries declined in the 1950s, the construction of the Samuel C. Moore Hydroelectric Station brought new vitality to the region, attracting professionals and providing hundreds of jobs.

In this scenic, active, and not-so-sleepy-after-all town, Littleton's beauty has entranced famous writers, poets, artists, actors, and musicians, including the likes of George Gershwin, Jascha Heifetz, Samuel Chotzinoff, Ernest Poole, Robert Frost, Eleanor Hodgman Porter, Nathaniel Hawthorne, Henry David Thoreau, Ralph Waldo Emerson, and Bette Davis.

But Littleton has yet another claim to fame: the hosting of sitting and would-be presidents. Since March 9, 1920, New Hampshire voters have been the first in the nation to cast their vote in every presidential primary. Littleton, and in particular, Thayer's Hotel—which in the '50s and '60s had the largest meeting space in the North Country—had been a frequent campaign stop for candidates of all parties. My parents' active roles in the Republican Party and their ownership of their business put them in close contact with every sitting and would-be president that came through during that time,

1 "QuickFacts: Littleton Town, Grafton County, New Hampshire," United States Census Bureau, accessed March 14, 2025, https://www.census.gov/quickfacts/fact/table/littletontowngraftoncountynewhampshire.

which meant I got to meet every president and every presidential candidate when I was growing up.

I have a picture of our family dog eager to jump on Richard Nixon as he posed in the lobby of Thayer's Hotel. When I look at that picture, I can still hear my parents saying, behind their smiles of clenched teeth, "Lucky … Lucky, get over here." There's a picture of me shaking hands with Nelson Rockefeller across the hotel's front desk and another of me waving my little flag at Dwight Eisenhower when he rode through town in an open convertible. Honestly, at that age, I thought everyone got to meet all the presidents—I didn't know it was unique to our little neck of the woods.

Likewise, I didn't realize at the time how unique it was that my mother, while raising me and running Thayer's Hotel in full partnership with my dad, served as president of Littleton Colonial Club (Women's Federated Club), the Profile Republican Women's Club, the Littleton Garden Club, and the Women's Auxiliary of Littleton Hospital. Later, after I was out of the house, my mother was appointed by President Richard Nixon to the United States Assay Commission and served at the Philadelphia Mint in 1970.

A few years after she had been appointed by President Richard Nixon, and then reappointed by President Gerald Ford, to the Department of Defense Conservation Awards Committee 1974–75, my mother was awarded an honorary medallion for serving on the National Defense Executive Reserve for the Department of Commerce. She also served on the New Hampshire Probation Commission 1974–1977, the Crime Commission's Correctional Study Advisory Board, the Crime Prevention Advisory Council 1976–1977, and the State Health Coordinating Council 1976—all positions she was appointed to by Governor Meldrim Thomson Jr.

(I know, a lot to live up to, right? I don't even try. And this is not even a complete list of my mother's achievements!)

My mother was, by anyone's standard, a smart and successful businesswomen, yet there was a business organization to which she was not allowed entry: the Littleton Rotary Club. Rotary International was for business*men* only—no women allowed. The first proposal to expand Rotary International beyond men was made in 1950 in India. But it would take another thirty-seven years before the first woman was sanctioned as an official member of the Rotary Club in the United States (a decision forced upon Rotary International by the US Supreme Court) and two additional years before Rotary International made its admission of women official worldwide.[2]

My dad was a member of the Littleton Rotary Club, and by extension, so was my mom, as she, ironically, was the one who hosted the club meetings in the dining room of our hotel. This was probably one of the first instances where I might have recognized the discrepancy in how men and women were treated in the business world, but my parents explained it to me by saying that it didn't make sense to have them both as members, so my dad was the Rotary member who represented the hotel. That seemed reasonable to me in my little childhood bubble of Thayer's Hotel, where everyone was believed to be equal, capable, and deserving of respect.

When, at the age of eleven, I began my first real job at the hotel, bussing tables, I was thrilled. Adults had jobs, and I so wanted to be an adult. My job in the dining room meant I was frequently in and out of the kitchen—an area of the hotel that was considered sacred. There was an established hierarchy in the kitchen, and it was not to be fooled with. The chef was in charge—period. If you didn't like

2 "Rotary History: History of Women in Rotary," Rotary, accessed August 2024, https://www.rotary.org/en/history-women-rotary.

it, you could work somewhere else. My parents had no tolerance for any kind of nonsense in the kitchen with its minefield of safety challenges, and my mother made sure every plate that left the kitchen was meticulously presented. The same held true for the hotel's three hundred–seat dining room. Every table was perfectly aligned with the others. Every server station was set up for high efficiency. Visually, everything was clean and orderly.

My mother was equally meticulous about our own presentation. She had her clothes made for her by a local seamstress—they fit her perfectly. I was required to be presentable as well, and so my mother had many of my clothes made, too. The snappy dresses she insisted on having made for me in my teen years didn't quite fit with the hippie culture of the '60s that I grew up in—I didn't own a pair of jeans until I was in college—but my fitting in with hippies was not her concern.

By high school, I had moved up from bussing tables to waitressing after school and on weekends. During our busiest season—which, in New Hampshire, is leaf-peeping season (foliage season) and occurs in late September, early October—I would walk down to the hotel during my lunch and study hall to wait tables and then walk back up the hill to school for my afternoon classes. I wholeheartedly believe that everyone should work as waitstaff at least once in their life; there is no better training course for managing a small business.

Waiting tables requires you to manage customer relations, timing, teamwork, and efficiency, all while being continually evaluated in real time by your customers, who will determine your compensation based on your performance. If you are waiting on four or five tables, you are essentially managing a small business. If a dish isn't right or the food isn't cooked correctly—two things you have no control over—you are still responsible for ensuring your guest is happy. You need to be able to anticipate issues, understand your guests, and think quickly on your feet. I don't think there is another position where your pay so instantly reflects how your customer feels about you. For a teenager, that's an invaluable lesson.

Hospitality requires attention and intuition. Colgate Holmes, founder of The Ritz-Carlton, told me they trained staff to mirror customer energy—if customers came in saying they just wanted to eat, staff knew to get dinner on the table ASAP, while if people came in relaxed and humorous, staff kept things casual. I realized that I had learned from the masters of intuiting customers' wants and needs—my parents. One time, my dad pulled me aside and said, "You know," nodding his head at one of my tables, "they came to have dinner with each other, not with you."

I understood immediately. I had not been attuned to my customers and had gotten too friendly. My customers didn't really care about how my summer was going or what I was studying. That was typical of how my parents taught me; they modeled expectations and shared observations. They rarely said, "Don't do this." Sixty years later, I still remember that simple and effective lesson.

Another pearl of wisdom that Colgate Holmes shared with me was this: Most hotel managers make the mistake of only focusing on the interior of their hotel, but customers decide how much they're going to pay based on their "sense of arrival," so paying attention to the exterior of the hotel is equally important. My mother knew that hands down. From the outside entrance to the restrooms to the back of the dining room and everywhere in between, Thayer's Hotel was visually appealing.

It was ingrained in everyone who worked at the hotel to pay attention—to check the entryway, restrooms, hallways, and lobby for anything amiss and straighten it out. If you saw something, you didn't think about it; you simply fixed it. It was just what you did, and my parents modeled the same care in the community in which we lived. You paid attention and checked on people when the weather got too cold; you shoveled the walkways and driveways of the people who couldn't do it themselves; you saw what needed to be done for the betterment of your community and the people in it, and you just did it.

I remember that, during my elementary school years, two high school girls lived with us on two separate occasions. At that time, we had moved out of the hotel and into a house. Both girls were waitresses at the hotel. I was not privy to the details of why they lived with us, but it seemed that my mother had concerns about each of their living situations and had decided to provide them with a safer alternative. These girls were several years older than me and were busy going to school and working, so our paths did not cross much.

By that time, I was already accustomed to people living with us. A couple of years earlier, my cousin and her family had been living with us while they were looking for a place to live. Again, I was never privy to the details of why people moved into our home—it just was. For a while, my grandmother lived with us, too. Even at home, everyone was respectful of the rules and each other, and no matter how many of us there were, meals were never a problem because they would all be cooked at the hotel and brought home.

My parents were smart, hardworking, and true partners in all things. They told me I could be anything I wanted to be if I was willing to work for it. While there were instances growing up that didn't appear "equal" to me—such as when my next-door neighbor, a boy my age, got on the Little League team, but I wasn't allowed (even though I was a much better softball player than he was)—I thought, *I guess they don't care about who has skill and who doesn't.*

> In 1972, President Nixon signed into law Title IX, which stated, "No person in the United States shall, on the basis of sex, be excluded from participation in, be denied the benefits of, or be subjected to discrimination under any education program or activity receiving Federal financial assistance."[3]

The passage of Title IX opened up athletics to girls, and in 1974, Little League rules were revised to allow participation by girls, which prompted the creation of the Little League Softball programs.

I grew up believing that how my parents lived and raised me was the norm, and I was happy to follow in their footsteps—footsteps, I would soon learn, that didn't always translate to the bigger world.

The inequalities that existed in the real world would come as an utter shock to me when I stepped onto the campus of Northeastern University to begin my studies in business. None more so than when the university handed me my first business school internship, as a cosmetics clerk at Filene's sales counter, while my fellow (male) students were assigned internships with banks, accounting firms, and other business school–appropriate placements. I was having none of their nonsense.

3 "The 14th Amendment and the Evolution of Title IX," US Courts, accessed January 2025, https://www.uscourts.gov/about-federal-courts/educational-resources/educational-activities/14th-amendment-and-evolution-title-ix.

Chapter 3

An Educated Woman

"You left off the turkey!" the chef said, as the breeze of a flying knife kissed my cheek. I turned to see the gleaming blade stuck in the wooden post just three inches from my head. "Understood," I said, and quietly turned and exited the kitchen. This was the summer internship I chose for myself when I turned down the cosmetic clerk stint the university had offered me. Putting the immediate risk to my personal safety aside, I knew I had absolutely made the right decision.

When my high school counselor had told me my only career options were nursing and teaching, I had known I was on my own. Neither of my parents had gone to college, so I could not turn to them for advice. A friend of mine was applying to Northeastern, so I decided to check it out. It had a business school with a pretty good reputation. It was in Boston, so not too far from home. *OK,* I thought, *I'll give Northeastern a try.* I applied, was accepted, and entered Northeastern as a freshman in the fall of 1967.

There were seven hundred men and thirty-three women in my business school class. In our first lecture, the male professor announced, "We have thirty-three trouble spots in this room, so would all the girls please move to the front so that those of us who want to learn will have the ability to learn." Yup, that happened. And all thirty-three of us did as we were told.

It gets better. The business school students were broken down into sixteen sections—sections fifteen and sixteen were then grouped together and consisted of the male students with the lowest SAT scores and all thirty-three female students. Northeastern's message was constantly made clear: Boys were there for an education, and girls were there for their MRS. I couldn't wrap my head around where this mindset—in a prominent educational institution, no less—came from. I grew up surrounded by women who could have run circles around any of Northeastern's male professors or students.

While my mother was my first fiercely independent female role model, she was not my only one. My dad's aunt, my Great-Aunt Evelyn, was a secretary in the Navy who was sent on a spy mission to Europe in 1939—my aunt was a spy! She and Dad both traveled to Europe on the *Queen Mary*. My dad's passage was on a troop ship with fifteen thousand soldiers in 1944. Aunt Evelyn never shared the secrets of her mission, no matter how many times my dad and I tried to get her to spill. Aunt Evelyn *chose* not to marry until she was sixty, which was just unheard of back then. My mom's sisters were also formidable women. My Aunt Imelda ran the family farm with her husband, who didn't speak English, as an equal partnership, just like my parents. When Aunt Imelda's husband passed, she ran the farm by herself—because she could. My Aunt Rhea ran the bar at Thayer's. Everyone loved Aunt Rhea, but they knew she was a force to be reckoned with if anyone thought about pulling any nonsense—there was never a question of who was in charge of the bar. I had grown up with female powerhouses and the men who supported and respected them, so the misogynistic environment I felt thrust into at Northeastern really was a shock to me.

When my freshman year was winding down, I was provided a summer work/study assignment as a cosmetics clerk at Filene's in Boston, making $1.10 an hour. Mind you, I was enrolled in their business school and had been on the dean's list for both semesters, and my male counterparts were coming back with assignments to the likes of State Street Corporation. Even without the inappropriateness of a placement as a cosmetics clerk for a business major, I wondered how I would even make that work financially, as I was paying my own way through school. My parents may not have gone to college, but they had made it clear from the start that I would, and (starting with my first job bussing tables at the hotel) every penny I had earned had gone into savings for my education. How would I support myself in a major US city on $1.10 an hour, even back in 1968? And it was a five-year program, so I would be paying for an extra year of school to learn to be a cosmetics clerk.

While I was trying to figure out my next steps, my dad asked me to come home and run the hotel for the summer. A couple of years earlier, my parents had bought a resort, The Crawford House. Located in Crawford Notch, about forty minutes from the hotel, it was one of the original grand resorts built in the 1800s. This five-hundred-acre resort with 160 rooms also included a golf course, a pond, a swimming pool, hiking trails, and more. While my parents ran the resort in July and August, they wanted me to oversee Thayer's Hotel.

Run a hotel or work as a cosmetics clerk? Seemed like a no-brainer to me, so I went back to the work/study office and proudly told the woman about my great alternative to the position at Filene's.

"We make the work/study assignments from this office," was her curt reply.

That was it for me, then. There was no way in hell I was going to pay for four more years to attend a university that thought so little of me and my female peers—one of whom had been an Israeli soldier in the 1967 war in Israel!

I wasted no time transferring to the University of New Hampshire (UNH), where I would begin in the fall, and I spent that summer managing Thayer's Hotel. I was seventeen, living at home alone, and running a business. I thought I had died and gone to heaven. Then reality hit. I opened the kitchen and dining room at six o'clock in the morning and didn't close them until ten at night, seven days a week. And of course, I had to be available for any guest or building issues around the clock.

I was also responsible for all the bookkeeping tasks, which came easily to me. I learned to create the daily spreadsheet by inputting numbers on the adding machine and then penciling the numbers into the desk-size ledgers, the original spreadsheet. (As meticulous as my mom was about the hotel, food, and uniforms, my dad was equally meticulous about the accuracy of the hotel's accounting records. I can still hear him saying, as he ran his finger down the columns, "Make sure all the numbers are aligned so you can add them up in your head as a check.")

Suffice it to say, there was not a lot of time for me to raise hell that summer (turned out my parents knew exactly what they were doing when they asked me to manage the hotel). It was midway through this summer that the chef's knife whizzed by my head.

As the person in charge, I was responsible for typing up the menu every day and making copies on the mimeograph. If an error was found after copies had been made, we would just handwrite the correction on each menu—that was easier than running all-new copies through the mimeograph. Unbeknownst to me, I had left off the special of the day, which, as you can probably guess by now, was turkey. The chef had been given a copy of the menu as soon as the copies were made; he had known the special was missing, but he had said nothing until I walked into the kitchen at the end of the dinner service that night and saw the fully cooked, uncarved turkey and all its trimmings sitting on the counter. I had disrupted his domain, and he made it perfectly clear that I was not to do that again—and I didn't. The kitchen had a hierarchy that you just didn't mess with.

When the summer came to an end, my parents closed the resort for the season and returned to the hotel, and I headed off to UNH. As a transfer student, I wasn't allowed to live in the dorms, so in the weeks leading up to the start of school, I had been looking for a place to live for me and two friends, one of whom I had been close with since kindergarten and who, almost seventy years later, is still one of my best friends. Initially, I found an apartment above a bakery, but then thought, *Living over a bakery, a person can gain five pounds by three o'clock in the morning just from the smell.* So, I abandoned what I realized was a dumbass idea. Also, the landlady thought we were hookers, so we hadn't made a great first impression …

I continued my search and discovered a trailer home for sale. It was the closest accommodation I could find to campus. Everything else was on the outskirts and would have necessitated us having a car—which we didn't have and couldn't afford. So, I talked my two soon-to-be roommates into coughing up $800 a piece, which was a lot of money at the time, and together we bought our first piece of real estate for $2,400 and lived there through the end of our senior year. With three years of "rent" paid up front, our only monthly housing expenses were heat, the trailer home park fee, and, of course, food, which unfortunately, we had to cook ourselves. Growing up in a hotel, my meals were always prepared by the chef, so I had never needed to learn how to cook. Then, when Frank came along, he did all the cooking. Suffice it to say, I have only a limited repertoire, although

I did learn to make a mean French toast in that trailer—the perfect cure for averting a hangover after a night of partying.

Over those three years, we learned how to live on our own and take care of ourselves, and since we owned the trailer, we also learned how to take care of our little piece of real estate. For instance, in the frigid winters of New England, pipes freeze if you don't pay attention—and that's especially true with trailer homes since they don't have a basement, leaving all piping exposed under the unit. There was more than one cold night in which, armed with a hair dryer, we took turns cramming ourselves under the trailer and blasting the pipes with hot air to keep them from freezing and subsequently bursting.

The university dorm dwellers were fascinated by our living situation. How had we managed to buy a home and still pay less than they were paying for their dorm rooms and food? We simply did what we had to do, and it turned out to be a great life lesson!

UNH turned out to be the right choice for me in so many ways. It provided me with a great education, it was half the cost of Northeastern, the campus and the classes were much smaller, and most importantly, I can't remember any differential treatment of the institution's female and male students. My days were straightforward, filled with classes, studies, work, and hanging out with my friends. I was fully engaged in my classes on economics and accounting, and I was glad that I had put the time and effort into understanding the material in my statistics course at Northeastern.

I had been terrified of failing that course because 90 percent of the students in my statistics class were taking it for the second time, and I thought, *I'm not going to do that.* So, I met with the professor almost every day after class to go through the material until I was sure I understood it fully—he probably figured the only way to get rid of me was to pass me!

That knowledge base was invaluable when I began my economics course. I learned then that if you need or want help, just ask for it.

I lucked out with my work/study placement at the UNH library shelving books. I could pretty much set my own schedule, and when my work was finished (since I was already at the library), I would usually get some studying done. The chief librarian was great to work for. She knew I was a good worker and would not shirk my responsibilities, so she gave me a lot of leeway. When she came around a corner and found me sitting on a stool engrossed in the book I was supposed to be shelving, she'd just chuckle and walk off. I appreciated the autonomy she afforded me, because trying to earn money while juggling your classes and studying and all the rest of it isn't always easy.

The culture at UNH couldn't have been more different from that at Northeastern. Maybe it was simply the difference between a big city school and a smaller one, or a large, private institution versus a small, public one. The bottom line is, UNH gave me access to an education and just let me get on with it. My business school cohort was a tight-knit group who really supported each other and had fun together. I was happy to party, but I was never one for big frat parties and had zero interest in joining a sorority. I tended to stick to my circle of friends, some of whom I went on long road trips with—driving to Daytona Beach for spring break and driving with a colleague to Vail and then on to San Francisco for Christmas break.

Amid our studies, parties, and road trips, the sociopolitical turmoil engulfing the US at that time would harshly remind us of the world outside our collegial bubble. The assassination of Dr. Martin Luther King Jr. in Memphis, Tennessee, on April 4, 1968, ignited riots in cities across the country, hastening the fight for and passing of the civil rights legislation that had been stalled in the US Senate.

Two years later, on April 28, 1970, as the opposition to the war in Vietnam mounted, President Nixon, without congressional approval, ordered US troops to invade Cambodia. His action served to intensify the anti-Vietnam war protests taking place on college campuses across the country. At the time, I was dating a guy in the Reserve Officers' Training Corps, and he called me one morning in mid-May and told me to stay away from campus because demonstrators and two members of the Chicago Seven, Abbie Hoffman and Tom Hayden, were en route to UNH, and the National Guard was circling the university. I understood his concern and heeded his warning.

To be a college student at that time was to know the dangers of student demonstrations. How could we not, after students were gunned down by the Ohio National Guard on the campus of Kent State on May 4, 1970, leaving four students dead and nine injured. It was just days after that tragic incident that my boyfriend had called with concern for my safety.

I did my best to keep my head down and focus on my studies, but reminders of the war and civil unrest were all around us. My neighbor a couple of trailers down was a young vet who, six weeks before starting at UNH, had been fighting in the rice paddies of Vietnam. There was no transitional help for these vets. In fact, the young men who had been drafted became the target of America's rage over the Vietnam war. Upon their return, they were often met with angry mobs, who yelled and spit at them and worse. The first time I went over to my neighbor's trailer, I knocked and then opened the door. He whipped around with his hand raised and then stopped. He hadn't heard my knock. "I could have killed you," he said. "Don't do that again." I didn't!

I graduated in 1971 from UNH's Whittemore School of Business and Economics (now the Peter T. Paul College of Business and Economics) with a Bachelor of Science—a necessity at the time if you hoped to get any white-collar job. My roommates and I also sold our trailer home for $2,400, returning to each of us our $800 investment. We had lived for three years *rent-free*. I thought, *I think there's something to this real estate thing*. That thought would eventually blossom into a full-fledged career in real estate, but first, as a newly minted college graduate, I needed to find a job.

Every job interview began with, "How many words a minute do you type?"

Every time, my response was, "I don't type."

I never applied for a secretarial position, and I refused to play the game. The best interview was with Abercrombie & Fitch. When I arrived, the interviewer took one look at me and said, "Oh, I'm sorry. I guess I forgot to tell personnel at the UNH Placement Office that we don't hire women." It seemed that more than a bachelor's degree was required for the white-collar jobs I was seeking.

I have never spent a nickel at Abercrombie & Fitch. Ever. That interaction was yet another moment in which I felt like the world had been turned upside down because, again, I had a front-row seat to the most competent businessperson I knew: my mother. And here, Abercrombie & Fitch had a policy of not hiring women, simply because they were women. And don't think they were the only ones; they were just one of the most candid about it. The truth became painfully clear: None of the recruiters that came to the campus were trying to recruit women for anything other than secretarial positions.

It was obvious that I did not have a lot of job prospects available to me in the business world. So, I came back home to Littleton and accepted a job at Littleton Savings Bank in the mortgage department. This unintentional landing was another piece of the puzzle that would lead me to real estate.

Chapter 4

Two Sets of Rules

My boss at Littleton Savings bank was a wonderful person to work for—he and I are still friends today. When I moved to Concord, New Hampshire, when I first got married, he recommended me to the mortgage department at New Hampshire Savings Bank. A couple of years later, the head of my department recommended me to be a senior loan officer, overseeing the lending department at Lowell Institution for Savings. During my interview, the president of the bank asked, "How much do you want to make?" Unprepared for such a question, I suggested what I thought was acceptable. He paid me more. A tremendous lesson for me: Acknowledging the value of your employees earns their loyalty. I would have worked twenty-four hours a day for him if that's what it took to do a good job. He also recognized my potential and wisely told me, "You will always be underestimated. Use it to your advantage."

That I would be underestimated was not an "aha" moment for me, but his message that I could use people's misperceptions of me to my advantage was. No longer was I offended when people underestimated me; instead, I watched and waited and took advantage at every turn. One of the best of such moments came years later, when I was chair of the board at Furr's. We were seeking outside corporate counsel and had begun interviewing firms. One of the interviews was with a large international law firm in Dallas, Texas. They had a breakfast buffet for us in the conference room, and as I was walking over to get my breakfast, one of the firm's senior partners came in and brusquely gave me his coffee order, in complete confidence that, as a woman, I must be a secretary. I smiled politely and headed off to fill it. If I hadn't been trying so hard to keep from laughing out loud, I would have had to kill him. But I knew that when he realized his error in the next few minutes, there was a good chance he would die of embarrassment without any help from me. When I set his coffee down next to him and then took my seat at the head of the table, as chair of the board, to begin the meeting, you could hear his jaw drop. He was speechless. His partners all looked a bit ill. It was a very short interview.

But long before that day, accepting the position of senior loan officer at Lowell was a game changer for me. I was the youngest senior loan officer in the US, and I was the first woman to serve on the board of directors for the Lowell, Massachusetts Home Builders Association (HBAs are trade associations that represent the interests of home builders, developers, contractors, and associated businesses). The association's annual fundraising project involved building a spec house, with the trades donating labor while we financed the materials. The project was fairly high risk for the bank, and as such, I felt it my responsibility to have a basic knowledge of what went into building a house. So, I told them that, in exchange for financing, they needed to provide me with the opportunity to be on-site and see the work being done every time a different trade was at the house.

That meant that when the foundation crew arrived, I was there to see how they put the formwork in and how they poured the concrete. The same was true when the framing, plumbing, electrics, siding, roofing, and any other work was performed. That knowledge became invaluable for me going forward as a mortgage and lending officer—I understood things that others would need to call on a tradesperson for. An additional bonus was that nobody expected me to know any of this stuff—who knew how much fun being underestimated could be?

The men on the HBA board of directors not only welcomed me to their building sites; they were also the first group of male colleagues who welcomed me onto their team and who, when needed, stood up for me. As a girl growing up in the '50s and '60s, I had never really learned how to play on a team, and certainly not on a team of boys. In elementary and middle school, girls weren't allowed to play sports. The only sport available for girls in high school was basketball, and (are you ready for this?) "because girls don't have the stamina to run the entire court," we could only play half-court. I wasn't interested. Now, as an adult, I knew that figuring out how to fit in with a team was critical for my career success, but there was no playbook that I could find on how to be "one of the guys" on the team—I was at a loss about how to fit in.

Turns out, I didn't need a playbook for the HBA team, because the guys on the board of directors were more than happy to show me the ropes. They taught me how to drink like them (no wine spritzers with that group), and I took to extra-dry martinis, straight up with a twist, like a fish to water. The group of them would go on trips, trips on which no women were allowed—this way, the guys could do whatever they wanted because their wives knew it did not include women. Well, one night, after an evening of heavy drinking in a bar in Boston, someone in the group decided we should go to Puerto Rico to gamble. Here, the details get a bit fuzzy, but I do remember airline tickets being bought, bits and pieces of our cab ride to Boston Logan International Airport, and more drinking on the plane. I also remember all the guys swearing that they would tell no one that I had gone on the trip with them—breaking the no-women rule would have created trouble with their wives, even though by this point I was considered "one of the guys." The next thing I knew, I was waking up alone in a hotel room in Puerto Rico with one hell of a hangover (oh, how I longed for some of my famous hangover French toast from my UNH days). It was one of the few mornings that I ever called in sick to work.

As desperate as I was to fit in, the HBA team were equally eager to teach me how "to live"—something they didn't think I was doing particularly well. If, by living, they meant randomly hopping on a plane at ten o'clock at night to go to Puerto Rico to gamble and regularly visiting strip clubs (they thought it important that I could distinguish a good strip club from a bad one, a skill I never actually found useful), they were absolutely right about my not knowing how to live.

While those may not all seem like appropriately supportive behaviors between colleagues, that's what the "good old boys" considered networking in those days, and it was their way of welcoming me as an equal member of their team. And I, for one, was thrilled to finally fit in. Most importantly, the guys willingly shared their knowledge with me, answering any question I asked, and they always, always had my back. I remember one night at the bar; I had mentioned to one of the guys that one of the other board members had been harassing me. The board was made up primarily of tradesmen—construction guys—and then a couple of vendors like me, the lender, and the insurance agent. The harasser was the insurance agent.

"I'm sure that's not the case," the HBA guy replied.

Well, I thought, *so much for their support.*

But, unbeknownst to me, the team began watching the insurance agent, and about a month later, at the end of another night of camaraderie, one of the contractors told me, "You leave when we tell you to leave."

"OK," I said, not thinking anything of it.

When they saw the insurance agent getting ready to leave, they told me to go too. Sure enough, as soon as I reached my car, the jerk shoved me against it and started grabbing my ass. Within seconds, the construction guys pulled him off me, shoved *him* up against the car, and said, "You bother Suzanne again, John, and we're going to rearrange your face for you." I was never bothered by John again.

My relationships with my team members within the bank were much more professional. We were a self-contained team, managing all the lending functions from mortgage approvals to collections, foreclosures, and repossessions. Building an aligned team is crucial to accomplishing goals. Following my parents' example, I set clear expectations of work and behaviors. That I was in charge of how my department functioned and that my team consisted mostly of women made achieving alignment a bit easier. Turns out women who work in a bank don't network like the guys—for which I was grateful.

I loved working with the HBA, and I loved the work my team and I were doing in the lending department. As I established my credibility, more opportunities came my way. It wasn't long after I arrived at Lowell Institution for Savings that I was asked to present at Savings Bank Association conferences. These conferences took me around the country and consisted of speaking to small groups of entry-level bankers who were looking for guidance and training on topics related to mortgages, lending, and leadership. This was another aspect I loved about my work with the bank.

In the midst of my time at Lowell Institution for Savings, my divorce from my first husband was finalized. And because I was now recognized in the banking industry on a national level, I chose to keep my married name. A name change would have made me disappear, forcing me to start to build a reputation for myself all over again.

I had been with Lowell Institution for Savings for five years. I was flourishing at my job. I was part of a team who welcomed and stood up for me. I had built my own team based on trust and respect. I was speaking across the country. I was hitting it out of the park on every front. I *loved* my job. Then, late one evening, I received a knock on my door. On the other side stood my boss.

"Hello?" I said cautiously.

He said, "I'm lonely." I was pretty sure he wasn't looking for someone to go with him to pick out a rescue dog.

I considered my options: send him home or sleep with him. I chose the former. I said, "You need to go home now."

He turned around and left. *Well,* I thought, as I thumped my back against the now-closed and locked door, *I have a car loan and a mortgage to pay, and tomorrow I'm not going to have a paycheck.*

The following morning when I walked into my office, it was empty, and I headed to the designated HR person. "What's going on?" I asked.

She stood up, and without looking at me, said, "I'll take you to your office."

I followed her to the basement, where she pointed toward a windowless room, then turned around and walked away without another word. It was one of the shittier moments in my life. I understood why my female colleague had offered no signs of support. She couldn't afford to be labeled a troublemaker. Women deemed troublemakers were blackballed, making it nearly impossible to find another job in their field. And it was never made clear what was considered troublemaking behavior.

People talk about a double standard back then, but the truth is, there was no double standard; there were simply two sets of rules. One for men and one for women. But the rules for women were never shared with you until the men in charge determined that something was a fireable offense. So, when you saw a female colleague fired for a certain behavior, you made a mental note: *That's considered trouble-making. Don't do that.* Although my boss had not technically fired me, he had created an untenable working environment for me.

If it hadn't been clear to me before, it was now: Fitting in with the culture, no matter how unfair and unethical, was seen as more important than work ethic or job performance.

My next career move, which was to Aetna, would play out similarly. I had a wonderful mentor; what I learned there would provide me with the confidence, knowledge, and opportunity to start my own successful business … *and* my professionalism would get me fired.

On the bright side, my move to Aetna would also mean a move to Hartford, Connecticut, where I would meet the love of my life, Frank Lord.

Chapter 5

The Only Skirt on the Golf Course

I teed up at the first hole while the other players (all men, of course) watched intently. I took a deep breath as I steadied my stance and adjusted my grip. *You just need to get off the tee without whiffing the ball or sending it into the woods. You can do this,* I assured myself. I focused my eye on the ball, raised my club, and swung.

As I watched my ball arc through the air, I allowed myself to exhale. It was a clean shot. A shot that set me up to par the first hole, and when I successfully putted my ball into that first hole, I couldn't help but smile. All that time Frank and I had spent at the driving range, putting green, and golf course preparing me for my first tournament had been worth it.

It wasn't by chance that I was the first woman invited to join the company's annual all-guy golf tournament. Bill Russell, my boss's boss, had made that happen, as only he, being a senior vice president (SVP) and the department head, could. When I left Lowell Institution for Savings, I landed at Aetna in Hartford, Connecticut. Being new to the area, I asked my coworkers whom I should talk to about getting involved in the goings-on in Hartford. "Talk to Bill" was the common refrain, and so I did. Bill was an active community member, and my taking the initiative to get involved in the Hartford community unintentionally put me on his radar. A few months later, when I was assigned to do a workout (an arrangement in which the loan obligations of the borrower, lender, or third parties are modified in a default situation or to prevent a default) at a Marriott hotel in Indiana, I landed on his radar again.

At Aetna, my combined real estate and hotel experience uniquely positioned me to see the difference between the two sectors. Insurance companies often maintain real estate investment portfolios; Aetna was no different, and its holdings included hotels. Generally, insurance companies viewed hotels merely as real estate (like office buildings or warehouses). They didn't understand that hotels were an operating business. They were used to office and retail spaces with leases and tenants that come up once a year for review, as opposed to the lease that comes up every night for a hotel renting out rooms on a nightly basis. And a hotel's restaurant operations are a separate operating business. The insurance companies couldn't understand how to restructure a loan to a hotel (i.e., how to do a workout) because they didn't understand that owning a hotel with a restaurant is completely different from simply owning a piece of property.

Bill saw the results of my Marriott workout. He saw my presentations to the investment committee. And he knew that there was nobody else in the department who could have pulled it off, regardless of any MBAs they had. I was the full package (without an MBA). Bill recognized the value that the marrying of my unique real estate and hotel acumen and experience could provide, and he chose to take me under his wing. Accepting that wing, I later learned, would ultimately lead to my firing.

But that day on the golf course had been well spent. Because it had been Bill who had put me there, I was in a protective bubble—no one was going to cause me any grief. I imagine that Bill also had a hand in whom my golf cart partner was that day—the head of construction services, who was a genuine gentleman. I remained 100 percent focused on my game, making sure I was ready when it was my turn to play. Both my dad and the golf pro I had taken lessons from had drilled into my head that what separates the good players from the horrible players is playing quickly. When you arrive at your ball, you get out of the cart, grab your club, and be ready to hit.

Once the last ball of the tournament had been sunk, I had a quick dinner and headed to my room. The mission had been to play a respectable game of golf, and that mission was accomplished. By this time, I knew to stay away from the all-male cocktail hours, dinners, and nights of drinking whenever possible—hanging out with the guys at Aetna was not the same as hanging out with the HBA construction guys. Glenda Reed, one of the few women at my level at Aetna, worked in the real estate division and served as a mentor during my time there. "If you have to go to department dinners or parties, get there early and leave early," she advised. "Otherwise, you see things you can't unsee, and you have to respect the people you work with in order to work with them."

It wasn't until years later, when a major construction company owner asked me to join them in a golf tournament, that I finally understood the lesson Bill had wanted me to learn that day on the golf course. The contractor who asked me to play had also asked along their future client, who would be paying them $100 million for his to-be-constructed building. I was behind that client in the foursome. He cheated on every hole. That was the lesson Bill had wanted me to learn: In five hours on the golf course, you learned the character of a person, gaining invaluable insights about your future business customers. In this case, I learned that cheaters cheat. Period.

As I watched the future client cheat, I thought, *Of course they asked him to play golf. They wanted to get to know him.* Now that they knew he was a cheater at something as inconsequential as a friendly golf game, the construction company would adjust their contract accordingly. They knew they would need more money upfront, more frequent billing, and likely a higher contract amount. What they learned from that five-hour block of time was invaluable to the success of their deal.

Bill recognized and respected my skills, abilities, and character. He saw my potential, but he also knew that I didn't fit Aetna's system. It was an incredibly broken system—at least in those days, as you will soon see—and one I was never going to fit into without comprising my integrity and values, something I was unwilling to do.

When I first began writing about my time at Aetna and recounting the unrelenting aggressions of my boss, I realized that, while I knew it had been bad, I had convinced myself that it hadn't really impacted me that much. It was just something I had had to put up with. But the more time I spent unlocking those memories, the more I was forced to acknowledge just how traumatizing the experience had been for me. As I reflected on that time, I also felt renewed gratitude that Frank had been in my life during those difficult years.

Frank and I met in 1981, a couple of years after I began at Aetna, and before long we moved in together, so he had a front-row seat to my struggles. How I was treated infuriated him. There were many nights when I would come home in tears, and Frank would be there to listen and remind me how incredibly capable and valuable I was and how wrong it was for me to be treated that way. To have no path available for me to address these wrongs without risking the loss of my job and possibly my career—not just because of the loss of income it would entail but because I would lose the work I loved and was incredibly competent at—was painful for both of us. And if I failed at Aetna after having to leave Lowell Institution for Savings, was there really going to be another chance, another career? I can laugh a bit now when I think of the evenings when I sat crying at the kitchen table, and after unburdening myself to Frank, he would say something lovely like, "How about I make you an omelet? Will that help?" Because good food was *always* the answer!

There was a moment in 1983, two years before I would be ushered out of Aetna, when I seriously considered accepting a job offer that would require a relocation to California to open Aetna's West Coast real estate office. When the move seemed imminent, Frank and I decided we should just get married before we headed out to the West Coast. The decision was all very practical; why make our family and friends trek to California for our wedding when we could just get married in Hartford? We didn't end up going to California, but we did end up married.

What I wanted from Aetna was simple: to do my job, to do it well, and to do it professionally. Bill had leveraged his authority to make that happen for me to the best of his ability, but my direct boss, David, made it increasingly difficult to accomplish.

I wasn't in the know that my credibility had eclipsed my boss's misconduct until years later. While he was the one who ultimately looked like the jackass, the experience was still humiliating and degrading for me. My ethics and stellar job performance could not save my job in the end, but fortunately, they did matter to the professionals I had worked with outside of Aetna (external partners, vendors, etc.), as was evident in the respect I garnered from them. Much to my boss's dismay, my stellar reputation in those circles eclipsed the influence of his bad behavior.

For example: San Francisco Bay Area was my territory, and it was booming. I was experiencing tremendous success. Then I went on a week's vacation. When I returned, I was informed, without explanation, that my territory had been switched to Indiana. Indiana was not booming. This was Lowell Institution for Savings all over again: I wasn't being fired—yet—but my boss was doing his best to sabotage my success and create an untenable environment for me to work in.

Three days later, my territory was just as suddenly switched back. I was happy to have regained the Bay Area and didn't ask questions. Years later, one of my California joint venture partners, who was a partner in the second-largest development company in the US at that time, asked, "Ever wonder how your territory got switched back so quickly?"

"Yes, I have," I said.

"Well, we called Bill Russell, and we told him you were responsive, you were smart, you paid attention, and you were who we wanted to work with." In the long run, securing my credibility with such partners was tremendously beneficial, but in the short term, the unfortunate truth was that the venture partner's call to Bill, which forced my boss to return my territory to me, was another nail in my firing coffin.

My boss's aggressions were varied and constant. When I submitted my list of accomplishments for annual bonus consideration, he returned it to me insisting that I cut it in half because my colleagues were men with families to support, so they clearly needed a bigger bonus.

When my boss told degrading "jokes" about women in staff meetings, as he frequently did, I would tell him after the meeting that his jokes were better suited for the men's locker room. His reply: "You just don't have a sense of humor."

I remember one meeting my boss and I attended with our San Francisco partners. He and I were the last to arrive, and just as we were about to walk in, he grabbed me, threw me over his shoulder, and carried me into the meeting. When he set me down, I felt as stunned as the partners looked. They glared at my boss, and then one of them said in a no-nonsense tone, "Let's get the meeting started, *now*." Like I said, it was my boss who looked like a jackass, but that made it no less humiliating for me.

My boss told me I needed to check in with him weekly. For six months, I documented my weekly attempts to do so and his weekly reply that he didn't have the time. That didn't prevent him from noting on my evaluation that I had failed to keep him updated on my work.

I'd like to say that my boss was the only person perpetuating this broken system, but that was not the case. When traveling for Aetna, I had male colleagues who tried to take me back to their apartments and who arranged business meetings at private clubs where Black people were not allowed or where women were dancing on the tables—I had no idea in advance what type of establishments these meetings were being held in, but after those two experiences, I made sure I did and refused accordingly. My male colleagues at Aetna socialized at each other's houses, but none of them was willing to invite a female colleague into their homes to meet their wives. I never fit in.

In between all the gross misconduct and alienation, I gathered valuable knowledge and skills and forged positive relationships on which I built my highly credible reputation.

The head of construction services at Aetna looked after my San Francisco Bay Area territory and was responsible for all of Aetna's $3 billion in equity real estate investments countrywide. We had a great relationship. He taught me to check specific things at a property and call him if he was needed. I learned the importance of 1) checking the maintenance room—if it was neat and orderly, that was a very good sign; 2) going on the roof—if there was ponding, there was likely a roof leak or soon would be; and 3) putting a ruler against the elevator cables—if it was flush with the cables, that meant the cables were worn. I found that after I demonstrated my knowledge of those three measures, people (i.e., men) frequently assumed I knew more than I did. It was a good learning experience that led to my wearing a thirty-foot, beat-to-shit measuring tape on my waist when dealing with construction guys. Today, when I go to Lowe's or Home Depot, or when I meet with contractors, I still wear my measuring tape on my waist, conveying that I don't need something as simple as a screwdriver mansplained to me.

My joint venture partners at Lincoln Property Company had all been fighter pilots in Vietnam. I learned quickly that not everyone viewed risk in the same way the investment division of an insurance company did! This was another positive and professional relationship. The pilots offered to take me on a helicopter ride over the Bay Area to show me future developments. This experience taught me how developers envision the future. We flew over the proposed highway exits, which was where they were buying up land. Easy on-and-off access to major highways is invaluable. My dad, I would later learn, had been a true visionary in much the same way. In Littleton, New Hampshire, as the manufacturing plants, shoe factories, tannery, and casket factory were moving out, he and other town leaders talked the town into buying 380 acres off the proposed Interstate 93 off-ramp and installing utilities. Today, in a town with a population of about 6,000, there are 1,600 people employed at the Littleton Coin Company, FedEx, Burndy, Harrison Publishing House, DirecTV, Spectrum, etc. Successful real estate developers and aspiring leaders must be able to see into the future.

At the end of the day, I realized that joint venture partners cared about one thing: executing real estate deals. Amid all the political minefields going off at Aetna, the one thing my partners knew they could count on was me delivering what I said I would deliver. One year, they called me in the beginning of December and said, "We need our partnership funding before year-end in order to make partner distributions." I knew that Aetna had a reputation for taking forever to do that, and I told them that I would do my very best to make it happen. Within a week, I was able to secure the partners $1.5 million. They sent me four dozen roses. The optics on that were horrible.

I called my contact and said, "Don't ever do that again, because doing so indicates special treatment, and me providing you with your partnership allocation in a timely manner was not special treatment." That is when I learned that it was common practice for many of my colleagues at Aetna to make clear what they wanted in return for providing the partner with what they needed, the delivery of which happened outside of Aetna. I didn't even know that was happening, and even if I had, I never would have played the game. I was compensated to do the job I signed up for, and I didn't want any special favors or major gifts as payoffs for simply doing my job. I remained focused on my career and continued to build my credibility with every step I took.

Chapter 6

I'm Good at Getting Fired

In the spring of 1985, I found myself engaged in what would turn out to be another significant day on the golf course. One of Aetna's national joint venture partners at Lincoln Property Company, who had been captain of the Stanford golf team and was a par golfer, suggested I go to California a day early so he and I could play golf at Pebble Beach with some of his other partners. This was a tremendous opportunity for anyone in my position, and I readily agreed. My boss was thrilled and gave me kudos for developing this critical relationship … Ha! While that is how my boss *should* have responded, and likely would have if I was a man, he instead saw it as the final transgression that would set the process of my firing in motion. Here's how it played out.

When I returned from California, my boss asked me to have coffee, a highly suspicious move. We hadn't had a weekly update meeting in over six months, let alone a coffee together (honestly, I can't even recall him engaging in a professional conversation with me—ever). As we sat down to have coffee, he gave me a memo documenting a meeting in which he had given me the required verbal warning. I read it and then pointed to the date of this supposed meeting at the top of the memo, and said, "Well, David, we both know you never gave me this warning because we never had this meeting, and it's particularly notable that we never had this meeting because I was in California on business for you on the date you're claiming we met."

He immediately reached to take back the memo. "No, no," I said, "I'll keep this," and I tucked it into my bag. Two weeks later, he officially fired me, a second VP at Aetna, for "insubordination, which is grounds for immediate termination" because "Ms. Hopgood accessed the department head, Bill Russell, without my permission."

My first stop was to Aetna's head of HR. I took the memo and a file of all my communications with my boss—most of which were my many attempts to fulfill his weekly meeting requirements and his consistent responses that he did not have time to meet with me—along with my documentation of every improper incident that had occurred during my five-year tenure at Aetna.

"What's in the file?" the head of HR asked, nodding at the very thick folder on my lap.

Any employee sitting in their office with a thick file of documentation is a nightmare for the head of HR. To make matters worse for Aetna's head of HR, the mid-to-late '80s were the beginning of a reckoning in corporate America, as Mechelle Vinson's sexual harassment case against Meritor Savings Bank was making its way through the court system, eventually landing in the US Supreme court in 1986.

In *Meritor Savings Bank v. Vinson* (1986),[4] the US Supreme Court unanimously ruled that sexual harassment that creates a hostile work environment is a violation of Title VII of the Civil Rights Act of 1964. The case concerned Mechelle Vinson, who brought an action claiming that her supervisor, Sidney Taylor, had subjected her to repeated sexual harassment, including rape, which she had not reported out of fear.

The lower courts had conflicting views, with the district court dismissing Vinson's claims based on the argument that the sexual relationship, if it had occurred, was voluntary. However, the Court of Appeals reversed this decision, establishing that such harassment could be actionable even if it did not result in a tangible economic loss and emphasizing that employers could be held liable for their supervisors' actions, even if they did not have direct knowledge of the misconduct.

The Supreme Court's decision confirmed that hostile work environment claims are valid under Title VII, focusing on whether the behavior was unwelcome rather than whether it was voluntary.[5]

"Well," I said, tapping the folder. "Every time something inappropriate has happened, I've made a note of it."

"Like what?" he asked.

4 Meritor Savings Bank v. Vinson, 477 U.S. 57 (1986).

5 David L. Dagley, "Meritor Savings Bank v. Vinson," in *Encyclopedia Britannica*, last modified June 12, 2024, https://www.britannica.com/topic/Meritor-Savings-Bank-v-Vinson.

I only needed to pull out two examples (which I came to refer to as "my two sticks of dynamite"). The first was my boss's requirement that I reduce my list of accomplishments because my male colleagues had families, and so they clearly *needed* a higher bonus. The second was the incident in which my boss threw me over his shoulder and carried me into a meeting with Aetna's joint venture developer partners. The head of HR looked at my folder again, then looked at me and said, "You have a good relationship with Bill Russell."

"I do," I replied.

"Do you think the two of you can work this out?"

"I'm pretty sure we can."

The following morning, I sat down with Bill to begin negotiating my transition out of Aetna. One of the first things Bill asked was whether we could agree that there would be no attorneys involved. I certainly didn't have the resources to take on a corporation such as Aetna, so not needing to hire legal representation was to my benefit. I was also fortunate to have a friend who was willing to help me to at least think through what I wanted the outcome to be, and he knew Bill well. So, when Bill asked for no attorneys, I agreed.

Bill also let me know that he had sent my boss out of town for the week so that we could negotiate without interference. And it did take us a week of morning meetings to work through the conditions of my transition. In the end, it was a two-page agreement that set me up for success and that Aetna could live with. While I'm sure negotiating my exit plan in a way that kept Aetna out of the papers and the courts was appreciated, Bill genuinely cared about how he could best help me. Shortly after my success with the workout at the Marriott in Indiana, Bill had pointed out that I could leverage my unique skill set to run my own business, consulting to corporations with hotel investments. These were the types of conversations we would have from that point forward—Bill's way of preparing me for the inevitable moment in front of us.

My good friend Bonnie and I have talked about this dichotomy of Bill being a genuine mentor to me, recognizing my potential and guiding me to a level of success that I could not have predicted, while simultaneously not being able to change the system's assault on women, which was too endemic for one department head to fix. A system that dysfunctional could only be fixed by a company's CEO, and even that was a challenge given the laws and the culture in the US at the time, which normalized all the bad behaviors as "boys will be boys." Done.

When I left, I was satisfied with my financial severance, but more importantly, I walked out with an Aetna recommendation, an Aetna background—which was better than an MBA—and an Aetna contract. All of which played a significant role in the launch of my consulting business, The Hopgood Group, LLC.

Within three years of leaving Aetna, two things occurred that gave me hope that someone was finally paying attention. The first was Frank coming home one night and telling me that the insurance company he worked for as an actuary, The Hartford, had just fired their highest-performing agent because he was having what he and his secretary said was "a consensual affair." Why was this big news? Because, as in nearly all cases of interoffice affairs, it was only the women who were disciplined, scorned, fired, etc. The woman was wrong, period, and the man kept his job without question or consequence. To fire the man in charge for being involved in the affair—and specifically, to fire a man who was bringing in the big bucks—was a huge statement. I couldn't believe it. And what a message that sent throughout the organization.

"Listen, Frank," I said, in all seriousness. "This company has ethics. You can't ever work anywhere else." (From that day forward, we also never bought insurance anywhere else.) The Hartford also instituted a new policy that took measures to curb the drunken misconduct (which most often led to the harassment of female employees) that occurred at department parties. The new policy made it clear that whoever was the highest-ranking person at a department party at any given time was the person responsible for any misconduct. Frank returned from one such party and told me how hilarious it was to see supervisors look around and realize, *Oh my God, I'm the highest-ranking person—I'm in charge,* and then run out the door as fast as they could. It was a brilliant policy—one that ended department parties a lot faster because that last leader standing would be quick to wrap the party up and send everyone on their way before it devolved into the usual shit show.

The second occurrence that gave me hope for change happened three years after my departure, when my former boss, David, made front-page news for his egregious behavior at Aetna's annual golf tournament. Around 1988, Aetna decided to include women at the annual golf tournament "for the first time"—my participation years earlier was still unknown. The male Aetna employees—with David as the senior staff member and ringleader—took magic markers and identified the hotel rooms occupied by the women by scrawling pictures of female body parts on their hotel room doors. The next morning, David and his crew arrived at the golf course with dildos strapped to their waists. Isn't that just hilarious? And keep in mind, these professionals—and I use that term loosely—were responsible for a $33 billion investment portfolio.

Unfortunately for David, one of the women had invited a friend who was an HR litigator, and she gathered the women together and informed them that they had the basis for a class action suit. The ugly details played out in the local newspaper; David was finally fired and transitioned to a job on the West Coast. I was thrilled to see him finally get his due, but I felt bad for his daughters, who were still in school, for having to deal with such an ugly, public exposure of their dad.

For all the positives that came from my time at Aetna, the trauma of my experience there took its toll. The combination of that trauma and my natural inclination to work until I dropped is what led to my significant health issues a year after my departure, which in turn led to my doctor emphatically telling me, "Suzanne, you have one of two choices. You go on vacation, or I put you in the hospital."

Two weeks later, Frank and I were on our way to Grenada. Turns out spending a week at a lovely resort (Frank even booked a room with its own pool!) is way more enjoyable than a hospital stay, and it accomplished my doctor's directive of turning off my work brain for a bit. Again, back then, when you went away, you had no choice but to be completely disconnected, whether you wanted to be or not—key for any workaholic like me. That forced disconnection was just what I needed, and it set us on our path of planning and enjoying regular weekend and annual getaways.

Chapter 7

Sometimes, You Have to Be a Badass

"So, how do I meet the big enchiladas?" I asked my dad, several months into starting The Hopgood Group. "I mean, I can't travel the country looking for clients."

My dad was a good Irishman with a great sense of humor. Once, he met a boyfriend of mine for the first time when they were both helping me move into a new apartment. My boyfriend's only job was to bring the beer, which he failed to do. "Well," my dad said, "looks like we won't be seeing him again." Turned out he was right. My dad was often right, and he was also a brilliant marketer.

"Let them come to you," he said.

"Oh, sure, and how do I get them to do that?" I asked.

"Host a conference and invite speakers. Everybody loves to be asked to speak; it makes them feel valued."

This was the most obvious thing in the world to my dad, but I was like, "Really? They'll come?"

"They'll come," he assured me. And they did. I couldn't believe how easy it was.

While establishing The Hopgood Group as a hotel consultancy (though my marketing people wisely steered me away from including that in the name, to allow for future expansion), I had developed a substantial mailing list from my real estate and Aetna contacts. This was the middle of the '80s, and due to a perfect storm fed by rising interest rates, overbuilding, economic recession, tax code changes, and the savings and loan crisis, real estate was in trouble, and hotels had it even worse. That meant that there were plenty of relevant topics about which real estate and hotel people were seeking advice, and my conferences would answer that need. My goal was to keep it simple: easy in and out for speakers and attendees, a one-day event, and highly focused on the relevant issue of the day.

First, I booked conference and hotel space at the Sheraton Hotel attached to Bradley International Airport in Hartford, Connecticut—easy in and out. Then, I identified the issue of the day and built a one-day conference around that issue. Next, I began calling CEOs and heads of marketing from the biggest hotel companies, explaining what I wanted them to speak on and the details of the conference. Everyone, unless they had a schedule conflict, said yes. I was stunned.

I marketed the event with brochures outlining the program, the speakers, and the number to call to sign up—in those days, the only delivery paths were the United States Postal Service and the phone.

That first year, I had a panel of fifteen hotel owners and management company executives who shared how they were navigating the economic downturn. I also had seventy-five attendees. I had the CEOs of big hotel companies flying in on their private jets to speak at my conference! My costs—the brochures, food, and conference space (I didn't have to pay the speakers; just as my dad had predicted, providing them a platform to speak was payment enough)—were covered by the attendee registration fee. I could not have come up with a more brilliant and successful marketing strategy—I really did learn from the best: my parents.

To take the strategy a step further, I decided to incorporate a speakers' dinner the evening before the conference. The speakers who were able to fly in the evening before joined me for dinner—I had all the heavy hitters to myself, and I made every minute count. Hospitality people love to gab, and these dinners were structured to stir opinions, forecasts, and friendly debate (remember what that used to be?). They were also an opportunity for me to get myself in front of hotel executives and make important connections. One year, the fire alarm went off in the hotel in the middle of the night, and we all got to see each other in our jammies. Not my best look, but good for a laugh. These annual conferences were my primary source of advertising for The Hopgood Group for almost ten years—by which time, my name had made national headlines on the "Board from Hell" in the inaugural edition of *Board Member Magazine.* But before I was launched into what felt like the lion's den, I poured myself into The Hopgood Group.

Outside of the conferences, consulting on hotel workouts (including the one at the Marriott in South Bend, Indiana, that put me on Bill Russell's radar for the second time) was my bread and butter. In fact, I was so valuable to the South Bend project that Aetna hired me to remain as the lead on it. But now, rather than as a second VP from Aetna, I would serve as a consultant from The Hopgood Group. There was no one else equipped to do what I did at that hotel, and Bill knew it—it was a win for both of us.

When I arrived the first time at the Marriott in South Bend, the hotel restaurant was experiencing significant losses, and it didn't take me long to figure out why. Often, hotels in college towns such as South Bend are developed based on the potential room rates and occupancy during family weekends, which means that all their numbers (their year-long pro forma) are formulated based on those highest-performing weeks of the year. Then they begin operating and realize that during some months of the year, there is nothing going on. During those times, not only is the hotel empty—so is the restaurant. Just as with the hotel, the hotel's restaurant was built to cater to parents, so the hotel had a high-end restaurant that college students were not frequenting on their own. No parents in town meant no patrons at the restaurant.

Aetna held the mortgage on the hotel, which meant my role was to keep the owners from defaulting on the loan, and the only way to accomplish this was to help the management company succeed in making the restaurant profitable. Hotel operations involve four key parties: the owner, the investor/lender, the brand name (such as Marriott), and a management company. Since property owners focus on real estate rather than operations, they hire specialized management companies to run their hotels' operations.

Here's how it unfolds. An owner buys the property with other investors and/or with a loan from a lender. The owner will then engage a management company, usually based upon whom the management company has a hotel brand affiliation with. For example, a particular management company may have a portfolio of Marriotts they manage, so they know Marriott's standards, brand requirements, etc. The owner must meet the brand's requirements in order to use and maintain that brand (e.g., if an owner wants to engage with The Ritz-Carlton brand, they will need to maintain the high-end glitz and glamour of a Ritz, with exceptional food and service, marble floors, spacious suites, and the like).

While the owner/investor/lender owns the building and the business, the management company controls all daily operations under the brand's requirements. So, if the hotel or its restaurant incurs losses, the owner must cover those losses without having any authority to make operational improvements or changes outside of the brand requirement. It's a challenging relationship, to say the least.

Now, if the owner wants to fire the management company, they can. But that would come with a whole lot of complications. There are significant cancellation provisions in a management company's contract, and the owner risks losing the associated brand if they violate any of them. Should this happen, the owner would need to find another brand to work with and a new management company. Depending on the brand, it can be difficult to make that switch. When you lose The Ritz brand, there are very few brands you can put in its place that won't be a downgrade, whereas moving from a Hampton Inn to a Comfort Suites or from a Red Roof Inn to a Motel 6 may not be so drastic but is still an incredible headache. A workout person like me is sent in by the owner or lender to try to improve the management company's success before the business is forced to default on the mortgage (in which case, the lender may foreclose and take ownership if operations don't improve and payments aren't made current) or the owner (where there is no mortgage involved) is at risk of incurring significant losses or losing the brand.

Bill Russell identified very early on that Aetna had no idea what its investments in hotels entailed. Then I came along, and he quickly realized that I knew mortgages and investments, but more importantly, I knew hotel management contracts, I knew hotel people, and I knew how hotels operated. I could go into the hotel's kitchen and identify problems instantly—from stolen food to improperly cooked fries. The look of surprise when this "banker" demonstrated such knowledge never got old. Bill recognized my unique value, mentoring me to leverage it in building my business, something I would never have figured out on my own.

The first thing I did when I met with the management company for the Marriott in South Bend, Indiana, was acknowledge that they couldn't be happy with the current situation either. "You're not doing well in this fancy restaurant, and we need to figure it out," I told them, and then I asked if I could meet with their restaurant people to strategize the best way forward. This was when I was still a second VP representing Aetna's $33 billion real estate department, and while the management company may not have been happy to see me, anybody I wanted to meet with was made available to me.

It was clear the hotel couldn't maintain a high-end restaurant 365 days a year, but in a college town, it could likely succeed with a pub-style restaurant. Liquor is a moneymaker, and a more limited and lower-end menu would significantly and quickly lower the hotel's expenses. A pub would enable both of those opportunities. I worked with the hotel for two years in my capacity as second VP and then continued for another two years as a hotel consultant for Aetna through The Hopgood Group, and we turned it around.

Because I understood how to accurately project occupancy rates and knew the inner workings of a hotel restaurant, the solution to convert to a lower-end restaurant and bar was obvious to me, and I was able to sell it to the management company. But sometimes, these negotiating dances are a bit more like a tango than a waltz. I remember one such tango, during my time as a consultant with the insurance company John Hancock. The current workout I was consulting on involved its bond division. Marlene, who headed a division in bond investments, was one of few women at her level in the middle of the '80s. Brilliant and all business, she respected and relied on my expertise. She and I did a lot of work together over the years. Marlene and her team were top-notch professionals and truly a pleasure to work with. These were common qualities among bond people, who often were regarded as upper-echelon people. Their offices were generally located on one of the top floors, above the equity and mortgage real estate divisions. I remember that the bond team was referred to as the "white shoe group," and the people on the team represented the highest performers from the top schools in the country. What they were not, however, was badass, so I gave them a front-row seat to how it's done.

This particular project involved owners who had defaulted on the hotel bond issue, which meant John Hancock was on the brink of taking possession and becoming the new owner of a portfolio of hotels nationwide—something it had no interest in doing. The current owners refused to be reasonable during our negotiations, and finally, it was time for me and my team to lay down the law.

"Listen," I said to the bond team at John Hancock, "I'm giving the owner one last chance to reach a deal, and this is how it's going to go. I'm going to make our final offer; he's going to refuse. When he does, I'm going to slam my files down on the table, stand up, and say, 'It's this deal or nothing. We're done here,' and then we're all going to walk out *together.*"

Their disbelieving faces continued to stare back at me. "It's going to be fine," I assured them. "You've all done the heavy lifting, and as a result, our legal standing is solid. Now it's time to call the owner's bluff and put a stop to all this drama." There were a couple of tentative head nods. "You don't have to say anything. You just need to stand up and storm out of the room with me. OK?"

There were more hesitant head nods and murmurs of "OK," but in the end, they all managed to play their roles perfectly, and it worked. The owners accepted our final offer, and we were finally able to eliminate the drama and get down to the business at hand.

"Sometimes," I told them, "you have to be a badass."

Chapter 8

You Can Work Any Eighteen Hours a Day You Want

I felt fortunate to have landed John Hancock as one of my first Hopgood Group clients, especially because I almost unintentionally ended the job before it got started. John Hancock originally hired me to analyze a hotel it had in Florida. Primarily, that task consisted of me completing a financial analysis that outlined what the hotel was worth and where I thought it was headed, but circumstances often required me to either renegotiate the hotel management agreement or replace the management company altogether. This workout took place amid the '80s real estate bust, when even well-managed properties and hotels struggled to stay afloat. Such was the case with John Hancock's Florida property.

Everything was in great shape except the market—something the hotel couldn't control. I saw no way to add value. Any honest summary I wrote would end simply with, "I'm sorry, but you're screwed." So, I called John Hancock. "Listen," I said, "I can't add value to this, and I'm not going to pretend I can. Let's just have you pay my travel, and we can cancel our contract."

There was a moment of silence on the other end of the phone, then a "Huh—I never had that happen before." I had momentarily stunned the representative with my candor, but in the end, they wanted me to complete the full analysis John Hancock had hired me to do. While I had no recommendations for improvement to offer, my analysis did provide the company with useful information, and my initial honesty had solidified my credibility. It wasn't long before I received a call from John Hancock's bond investment department, seeking my services once again for a hotel portfolio workout.

John Hancock had a portfolio of hotels in the greater Boston area that were in default, and it wanted my help in taking possession of them. Like executing a search warrant, my work began only once legal gave the all clear. Once I had all the documents in hand and the new management company ready to take over, I informed the general manager of the change in ownership, collected the safe combination, and asked the manager to leave. While tense, it's typically a straightforward process since they'd been advised this was coming. This possession turnaround took four days working 24/7.

The priority out of the gate is always to inform the employees that they all still have a job, they will still get paid, and that the hotel is still open for business—the only difference is the manager. Because I was a hotel person, I spoke the employees' language, and I understood their concerns. This helped make for a smoother transition. You'll never believe what the next priority always is: pouring every drop of alcohol down the drain. When ownership changes, the current liquor license is no longer valid. It is painful pouring bottle after bottle of single malt scotch down the sink, but it must be done. When the new liquor license is obtained, the restocking of the bar begins.

John Hancock became one of my largest Hopgood Group clients. Over the years, I did work for their mortgage and equity real estate department, bond investment, and legal divisions. It was a great relationship based on mutual respect, one that would eventually propel me onto the national stage in an unexpected way—but that was still a few years down the road.

Mellon Bank was another Hopgood client that I landed courtesy of Bill Russell. As real estate frantically tried to rebound, the banks, in their attempt to not go down with the ship, were busy separating their bad assets from their good ones. These bad assets would be moved to a newly formed independent national bank for liquidation (often referred to as the "bad bank") so they would not have to be reported as part of the primary bank's assets. In 1988, Mellon Bank became the first bank to institute this strategy.[6]

I never fully understood the "bad bank" strategy, but I was part of a workout with Mellon Bank that involved this separation of assets. Robert Parkinson was the head of workouts for Mellon Bank, and he hired me because Bill Russell had told him that Mellon didn't know how to deal with hotels. What was different about these "bad bank" workouts was that the primary goal was to stop the bleeding as quickly as possible so that the asset would be a more appealing property for someone else to own. Mellon Bank had zero interest in trying to turn these failing assets around—it simply wanted out with the least pain possible. That might involve something as simple as closing the restaurant for lunch every day, which would immediately reduce payroll, food costs, etc., enough to tip the balance sheet from red to black.

Robert was 100 percent focused on the task at hand, and he moved fast—which worked well for me. He was brilliant at what he did, and we learned a lot from each other. Robert had the hotel's

---

6 Gabriel Brenna et al., "Understanding the Bad Bank," *McKinsey on Corporate & Investment Banking* 9 (2009), https://www.mckinsey.com/~/media/McKinsey/Industries/Financial%20Services/Our%20Insights/Understanding%20the%20bad%20bank/Understanding%20the%20bad%20bank.pdf.

financials, so we knew where the significant issues were in advance. The goal was to check out the operations without identifying who we were and why we were there—and this made for some funny moments. We would approach reception and ask if we could see a room (it may have been under the guise of planning a future event that necessitated us reserving a block of rooms), or we might eat at the restaurant.

I remember one of our first trips to a hotel in Houston. We arrived at the front desk, and I said, "We'd like to see a room, please."

"Oh, are you married?" the receptionist asked (remember, this was the '80s).

"Yes," I said, at the same moment that Robert said, "No."

I gave him a side glance and then smiled at the receptionist. "It's confusing," I said. Robert and I had a good laugh about that one.

From that point forward, I insisted we get our story straight in advance and that I do most of the talking—as the hotel expert, I had all sorts of questions when looking at rooms and dining in the restaurant that would help me figure out where we could make the quickest difference without giving away what we were up to.

Robert understood the rules by which the bank had to play. That was something I had to learn for various clients: What bodies were they governed by (such as the Securities and Exchange Commission [SEC] or the Federal Deposit Insurance Corporation)? Every organization had various governing bodies it had to report to, and I had to understand how those rules impacted how that organization could do business so that I could make recommendations that had value.

Robert taught me about optics. As consultants, we had to pay for our own hotel rooms. At one point, when I mentioned getting a better rate at The Ritz-Carlton than the Marriott, he replied, "I will never submit an expense report from The Ritz-Carlton. It's bad optics.

The client never gets to the charges because all they see is that I stayed at The Ritz-Carlton." He was right, and I was grateful for the insight. Working with Robert was a wonderful experience.

As my Hopgood clientele grew, I was up to my ears in work. I quickly realized that when you work for yourself, you can work any eighteen hours of the day you want. While my days often ran from four o'clock in the morning to ten o'clock at night, Frank maintained a better balance, even as we both pursued community involvement—a driving force for both of us.

I began my community work as a member of the Hartford Downtown Council, a position I acquired courtesy of Bill Russell. Bill recommended me because he thought at least one person on the council should be someone who actually lived in downtown Hartford. It was typical back then that the suburbanites of Hartford thought that the city needed their outside direction telling us how to run the city because, to their thinking, nobody in their right mind would choose to live in the city. Most of these individuals represented corporations that had headquarters in and around the area. Over time, the board members expanded how they thought about what a vital downtown should look like, which—guess what—included making it livable, not just workable. Years later, I was proud to chair a board that added three thousand apartments to downtown Hartford with a 92 percent occupancy.

Around that same time, Frank became a board member and, subsequently, president of the Mark Twain House and Museum in Hartford. Frank had chosen this board because it was in the neighborhood we lived in, and he thought a neighborhood resident should be a representative on the board. Just as he was transitioning to being board president, the executive director of the Mark Twain House left. Taking on the role of board president of a nonprofit that just lost its executive director is no joke (especially when you still have a full-time job), and Frank threw his heart and soul into it for several years, as a board member and, in later years, as a trustee. Even after Frank's passing, his heart and soul remained entwined with the Mark Twain House and Museum, recognized through the dedication of the Frank C. Lord Welcome Desk. This was a beautiful tribute to Frank that represented his welcoming spirit and care and concern for his community.

Between work and community commitments, Frank and I were both incredibly busy during the week, which made those weekends in Old Saybrook, Connecticut, so critical for us. Friends of ours had introduced Old Saybrook to us shortly after Frank and I met, and we had fallen in love with it. Just a forty-five-minute drive from Hartford, in the early years of our marriage, we would drive down there on Saturday for the day, return home, and then do the same on Sunday. That's how we had learned to play golf in preparation for my entrance into Aetna's golf tournament. Then, in 1983, shortly after we were married and during my time at Aetna, I was feeling the pressure at work and a real urgency to get away for the whole weekend, rather than just for day trips, so we began looking to buy a home of our own in Old Saybrook.

We found a house sitting on three-quarters of an acre of waterfront property. The beneficiaries of the property were trying to decide between hiring a broker and leaving it with the bank to sell. As a result, it wasn't open to standard showings. Our broker said, "They haven't made a decision yet about what they're going to do, so I can only get you in the house for ten minutes." That was all I needed. The value was in the land, but I needed to make sure we could live in the house during any renovations we needed to have done. Thanks to my knowledge gained through my work with the HBA (I keep all the lessons I learn along the way in my back pocket, ready to be pulled out when needed), I could determine the house's livability in ten minutes. It was livable, and as soon as the property was ours, it became our weekend retreat, every weekend for years, and is now a summer retreat for me.

We would head to Old Saybrook on a Friday evening and stay until Monday morning. I was never going to be the person who worked forty-hour workweeks (who am I kidding? I was never going to be the person who worked less than an eighty-hour workweek; Frank and I both knew that), so my disconnecting on the weekends was essential to my mental and physical health.

The other thing Frank and I were committed to was regular exercise. When we met, we were both runners, as in six miles per day—I was a morning runner, because no one wants to talk to you at six o'clock in the morning. We both kept that up until we began to have knee issues. I think I was the first one to give up running, and in search of a replacement, I found biking. My newfound exercise eventually led to Frank and me biking all over the world—we absolutely loved it. Our first international biking trip was in Austria in 1998. For that, we joined friends on a scheduled bike trip, during which we learned what we *didn't* want. The bike group leaders made us all stay together, and with everyone biking at different speeds and stopping for water or pee breaks at different times, it just wasn't as enjoyable as it could have been.

From then on, a member of our local bike group managed the when and where of our trips. He was an architect with an incredible talent for charting routes and finding great places to see and stay. Every trip he coordinated was amazing. We each had trip responsibilities. Frank's job was to find the best places to eat—which he was phenomenal at doing. My job was to ensure that our luggage (or, as we learned to call it, our "baggage"—a word that, while it might be pronounced differently, is the same all around the world) was transported between hotels. This often involved pulling out our itinerary and pointing to the location of our next destination while simultaneously engaging in a variety of hand gestures. It never failed that the desk clerk, no matter where we were, knew a family member who would take our baggage to our next hotel for a small sum. Thankfully, our baggage always arrived exactly where it was supposed to.

In the initial years of our biking adventures, airlines shipped our large, heavy bike boxes for free. Years later, they began charging a $500 fee, and that was the end of Frank and me transporting our own bikes. When we looked back at pictures of when we used to spend hours taking our bikes apart and then putting them back together, we wondered, *What were we thinking?*

Remember how I told you how painfully (and I do mean painfully) honest Frank was? Well, one time, we were flying back from one of our biking vacations and had packed our bikes in one of the big bike boxes, which took about a day and a half to do. At the airport, the woman at the counter asked, "Did you deflate your tires?" and I thought, *Oh my God, I can't let Frank answer!*

"Yes, we did," I blurted, and moved Frank along as quickly as I could. All I could think was, *If I let Frank answer, he's going to say no, and we're going to miss the damn flight to spend the day unpacking and repacking our bikes.* "A tube blowing because our tires are inflated," I assured him after our bikes were checked in, "will not bring down the plane."

We biked in Italy, Spain, Austria, France, and Germany for many years, and no matter where we arrived, people were incredibly friendly. When you arrive as a bike rider, people understand how challenging it is to get yourself there, and they just welcome you in with open arms.

In 2013, in part due to our interest in seeing what we referred to as "big rocks," we began biking through parts of Asia. Our first big rock sighting had been while on our honeymoon in Mexico, where we visited Chichén Itzá, and now that interest would take us to the other side of the world.

January 2013 found us, on our 29th anniversary, in Vietnam. A friend, who had been an Army Ranger in Vietnam, and his wife had biked through the country with SpiceRoads Cycling. I asked how it was. He replied, "It's a beautiful country when no one's shooting at you." Frank and I opted for the Saigon-to-Bangkok bike trip with SpiceRoads, which started with a bike ride from Saigon to the Mekong Delta; a boat trip on the Mekong River, crossing the border into Cambodia; biking to Phnom Penh, Cambodia; then on to one of the top UNESCO sites in the world: Angkor Wat.

It was amazing to ride through this beautiful country with a group of people from around the world who also loved biking their way to and through amazing sights. Our final stop was at a resort on the border of Thailand. We learned that SpiceRoads always ended its trips at a fabulous resort, and we were grateful for the extra five days our resort stay gave us to recover. The food was amazing, and we developed the phrase, "We bike to eat." We knew that if we were going to keep eating like this, we would have to keep biking!

This inaugural trip in Southeast Asia would lead us to Thailand and Myanmar (formerly Burma), as well as to India and Sri Lanka in South Asia. Of all our destinations, Thailand would be the one that captured our hearts. Frank and I biked through the country in 2017 and 2018. Thailand has a fascinating history, remarkable Buddhist temples, and incredibly kind and friendly people who couldn't seem to do enough for us ... And the *food*!!!! So enamored were we with the people, culture, and landscape of this amazing country that when we booked our 2019 trip to Thailand, we decided we would no longer rent bikes on location. Instead, we planned on buying our own bikes in Thailand so we would have them on what we knew would be an annual trip for us. But the 2019 trip was not meant to be. I wouldn't return to Thailand until 2023, another first without Frank.

Our international biking adventures were how we chose to spend our big annual vacations, but my work also allowed us to travel the world (without bikes). A lot of those trips were courtesy of my work with the National Association of Corporate Directors (NACD), which I will share in more detail later. The NACD flew me to Moscow, Hong Kong, São Paulo, Rio, and Beijing, and Frank came along on a "companion ticket." While I was busy working, Frank was busy seeking out the best places for us to see in the afternoons and evenings, and he always found us the best places to eat. Not the most expensive—that would have been too easy. He would go around reading the menus of all the restaurants and, without fail, find us the most delicious food. We loved discovering new cuisines together—I'm not talking insects or rats here, but we were both willing to venture into unknown territory.

On those trips, Frank got us into places that I wouldn't have dared go to. But it was so much more than that. Frank slowed me down long enough to experience the world beyond the scope of my work. When I realized I could work any eighteen hours a day, it wasn't dread that I felt; it was glee about all the work I could get done in that time. If not for Frank, I would have flown in, done the work, and flown back out to do more work. Seeing the world through Frank's eyes was one of the many ways he enriched my life. Traveling with Frank was always a true joy, and whatever interesting place he found for us, I willingly followed, even if sometimes naively. One time, we were in São Paulo, one of the most dangerous cities in the world, for a conference where I was the keynote speaker. I remember sharing on a call with the head of the conference that Frank and I had been riding the subway system, and she replied, "Stay in your hotel. I'm going to send a car for you in the morning, and you'll stay at my condo on the beach."

When I hung up, I said to Frank, "I think she wants to make sure her keynote speaker doesn't disappear, never to be found again." We had a good laugh over that one and reported to the condo the next morning as instructed—it was fabulous.

We did quite a bit of traveling across the United States as well. It's funny how, even when you have traveled the world, it is sometimes the most ordinary of places that are the most eye-opening. One of my jobs landed me in Lubbock, Texas, and for the better part of two years, I frequently flew home to Hartford, and Frank would spend time with me either in Lubbock or in the other US cities my work required me to be in. For a small-town New England girl, landing in Lubbock was like landing in another world.

Chapter 9

Yes, You Are Putting That on Your Résumé

"We won the proxy contest," said the Teachers Insurance and Annuity Association of America College Retirement Equities Fund (TIAA-CREF) representative on the other end of the phone, followed by, "You need to go in as chair." TIAA-CREF's governance department was a leading governance advocate at the time and highly respected throughout the investment world, and the workout division had initiated this (one and only) proxy contest.

I hesitated, then said, "Here's the problem with that. The CEO says he's quitting if you take over."

"Well, I guess you're going to have to be chair and CEO."

"When do I have to let you know if I accept?" I asked.

"I'll call you back in three hours," said the representative.

I hung up the phone, momentarily stunned, and then my mind began to race. *I've never been a board chair or a CEO, never mind for a NYSE company. I've also never run a public company. I've never run a restaurant company with five thousand employees. And,* I then thought, *if I was a guy, I wouldn't be worrying what I haven't done. I'd be asking, "How much are you going to pay me?"*

I immediately called my colleague and friend, Rachel Roginsky. "Rachel," I said, "TIAA-CREF wants me to be chair of Furr's *and* interim CEO. But how can I? I have a business, employees, contracts, commitments, obligations—"

"Suzanne," Rachel interrupted me, "this is a fantastic opportunity. You can do this, and you absolutely must do this. Do you know how many female chairs and CEOs are running New York Stock Exchange companies? Not enough."

"But I have employees, clients, contracts …" I repeated.

"Suzanne, listen to me. The titles of chair and CEO of a New York Stock Exchange company are going on your résumé. I will run The Hopgood Group until you fill the CEO position. Tell your employees they'll be reporting to me for now. I'll do the work, and you can deliver the results to your clients in person," said Rachel, and she did for a full year, all while running her own Boston-based business.

Frank was with me when I got the call. Like Rachel, he was emphatic that I needed to take this opportunity, that I would figure it out. Then he said, "And it's not just the fact that you're a woman. How many New York Stock Exchange chairs and CEOs are only forty-eight years old?" I'm so often amazed at the utter confidence people have in me to do what I have never done before.

And that is how, on Thursday, May 28, 1998, I became chair *and* interim CEO of Furr's/Bishop, Inc., a NYSE company—two roles, I might add, that should never be held by the same person. When that happens, the checks and balances that the distinct roles of board chair and CEO are meant to ensure are put at risk. The board's responsibilities involve governance, setting the firm's strategic direction, and fiduciary oversight. The CEO is responsible for executing that strategic direction through the day-to-day operations of the organization. The only employee that the board hires, fires, and manages is the

CEO, so having a CEO also chair the board that oversees their own role is a direct conflict. This is a drum I continued to beat beyond my time at Furr's, including when I was hired as a governance expert representing institutional investors and introducing and/or supporting resolutions that were being presented at shareholder meetings. I gave one such presentation to chair/CEO Bob Igor of Disney at the Disney shareholder meeting (accompanied by a certain one-eyed monster and other Disney characters). Another I gave at the J.P. Morgan shareholder meeting, where I spoke directly to Jamie Dimon, chair/CEO of J.P. Morgan, telling him that my client thought he was doing a great job, but they wished he had one job to focus on, rather than two.

Fortunately for Furr's, I knew what the checks and balances were and was committed to ensuring they were maintained despite my dual roles, but I had no desire to walk that tightrope for long. Thankfully, my roles as chair and interim CEO were brief (two years as chair and one as CEO), but they sure packed a punch. From firing the chief operating officer (COO) right out of the gate to discovering that the company, unbeknownst to the board or shareholders, was mired in a class action suit to relocating the company headquarters out of its hometown of Lubbock, Texas.

Landing in Lubbock was a culture shock for me. "What church do you go to?" was one of the first questions I was asked when I arrived in Lubbock. I'm a New Englander; we're not the friendliest people. What we are is private people. In Littleton, New Hampshire, nobody ever asked what religion you were or what your political affiliation was. If someone shared that information, that was all well and good, but never would anyone be so brazen as to ask, and certainly not upon first meeting you. But there it was. I was so stunned I just mumbled something like, "I really haven't gone to church here yet." During the period in which I was a frequent flyer between Lubbock and Hartford, the question was changed to, "Did you make it back from Hartford in time to go to church?" My natural inclination was to say, "None of your damn business," but I held my tongue and just stated the time when I had returned ("I got back around three o'clock"—or one o'clock, or whatever time it was) before quickly moving to another subject.

Here's the other question I was asked shortly after arriving in Lubbock: "Do you know what to do in a tornado?" My response was a nervous, "No," after which I was provided the following instructions: Go into a windowless room and pull a mattress over your head. "Well," I said, "if you've got a king-size mattress, you've got a problem, apparently."

Then there was Furr's $6 all-you-can-eat cafeteria-style restaurants that I was now responsible for. These low-end buffet-dining experiences just didn't exist in the northeast at that time, so the concept was completely foreign to Frank and me. And, as you can guess, $6 of all-you-can-eat food is, well, the grade of food that $6 can buy. As I shared, Frank and I loved good food—and this wasn't it.

One of the first things Frank asked was, "Do we have to eat there?"

"I'm the CEO, Frank. Yes, we have to eat there."

And finally, there was the drastically different geography and climate. Spring ushers in the ongoing threat of tornadoes, and summers in Texas are extremely hot, with the occasional dust storm kicking up for good measure. The ocean was a full day's drive away from Lubbock, and the lush foliage of New England was nonexistent. Like I said, it was like landing in another world.

Furr's would end up setting a precedent as the first institutional investor (in this case, TIAA-CREF) to replace a sitting board of an American corporation. As a buffet chain that boasted one hundred restaurants serving thirty-two million customers a year in fifteen states, it also had a commissary, a trucking operation, and a meat-testing facility, all based in Lubbock, and I was now, as chair and CEO, doubly responsible for all of it.

While my positions on the board were new, I was not new to the Furr's board of directors. Two years prior, in 1996, in response to Furr's defaulting on its debt and a negotiated debt-for-equity swap in the company, John Hancock had recommended me as a director to the Furr's board. Those first two years with Furr's had packed their own punches. The board's extreme dysfunction led to the inaugural edition of *Corporate Board Member's* magazine article, "The Board from Hell." Not really the type of publicity I was seeking as the face of The Hopgood Group (although the article presented me as the most civil member of the board), but in the end, my role with Furr's elevated me to a national level that opened doors I could never have imagined walking through.

The "Board from Hell" years were filled with power struggles, infighting, and board members forcing themselves into the company's day-to-day operations—its members got so far into the minutiae that, at one meeting, they fought over the color of Jell-O to be served (the CEO was so fed up that he took Jell-O off the menu).

All this dysfunction and poor leadership led to declining sales and the eventual default on the company's debt. This eventually culminated in TIAA-CREF's workout division launching its only proxy contest to replace the board with its own slate in what *The Wall Street Journal* reported as "the shot heard round the world."[7]

TIAA-CREF had its own slate of board members ready if it won the proxy contest. When it did win, it surprised me with the chair

7 Ellen E. Schultz and Susan Warren, "Pension System Ousts Company's Board in Big Victory for Institutional Investors," *The Wall Street Journal*, May 29, 1998, https://www.wsj.com/articles/SB896313163520654000.

and CEO request. The new board members—all men and all workout people like me—were all unknown to me, except for one holdover from the previous board. At our first board meeting, as part of the board's election responsibilities, the members had to formally elect me as chair and then as interim CEO when the CEO resigned. "I am totally opposed," I assured them, "to having two very distinct jobs in one, and you will not receive any pushback from me about hiring a CEO. But this is what we are working with now." I also made it clear that, in my distinct roles, I would not share any operational information with board members that, as CEO, I did not think was relevant to them. And that was my first action as chair.

My first action as CEO was firing the COO, Jim. I had been informed that he had poked a restaurant manager in the chest hard enough to leave a bruise. I don't condone assaulting employees, period. Before I met with Jim for what would be his termination meeting, I asked around about him. The last thing I wanted to do was fire somebody and then have the whole senior team leave. I knew from experience that when you walk into what I was walking into, it's critical that you quickly figure out where your resources are. Fortunately, there was a long-time employee who was highly competent and well-liked and who understood the whole operation. He had also previously been a COO. I asked him if he could take over when I fired Jim, and he said he would.

I then called Jim into my office and told him that we wouldn't be needing him anymore, so he could pack up his stuff and leave. That's the other thing we New Englanders are—direct. We like to get right to it—no point in wasting time on preamble or small talk.

"I don't think you can do that. You're not a real CEO," Jim said.

"Well, we'll see how that goes for you," I replied in my best badass voice.

He stood there for a moment, and I added, "You should probably start packing up your stuff from your office, and if you need help, the head of HR can help you." It didn't hurt that the head of HR was a retired marine.

Jim left, and I never heard another word from him.

To wrap up the end of my first week as chair and CEO of Furr's, the chief financial officer (CFO) came into my office and said, "There's something I don't think you know that you need to know."

My first thought was, *I'm pretty sure this is not going to be, "We have more cash than you thought."*

"We have an undisclosed class action suit," he continued.

"Oh, that's a problem," I said.

As soon as I understood that the suit fell under the Employee Retirement Income Security Act of 1974 (ERISA)—a federal law that establishes minimum standards for most voluntarily created retirement and health plans in the private sector, ensuring protection for the individuals enrolled in these plans—I knew this was no simple slip-and-fall suit. When I began working at Aetna in 1979, ERISA was in full effect, and during my time there, I became extremely well-versed in it. I knew this suit had legs—it was serious.

As a NYSE company whose shareholders were not privy to the material information related to this suit, we could not legally continue trading on the stock exchange. I immediately called our outside counsel, who called the SEC to stop the trading of Furr's/Bishop, Inc. shares. My next step was convening a board meeting for Saturday morning, which is a clear signal of crisis. At that meeting, two of the board members took on the task of finding out the details and seriousness of the suit. Until we could understand the issues, draft a release disclosing the suit, and fully inform all shareholders, our trading on the NYSE would be at a standstill.

I knew with Furr's that I was walking into a firestorm, which made my standard practice of identifying the top five priorities even more critical. While companies have many important priorities, tackling more than five at once overtaxes resources, and nothing gets done. Proper allocation of resources is the CEO's number one job.

As CEO, I identified the top five priorities for Furr's/Bishop, Inc.:

Identify immediate issues (the class action suit, filing an SEC disclosure, liquidity, and food safety).

Prioritize those issues and determine how to address them.

Review the leadership team and find replacements as needed.

Identify "success" (for instance, is winning a lawsuit that costs twice the disputed amount in legal fees considered success?).

Determine what the restaurants see as their biggest challenges and develop a plan to overcome them.

Some of the tasks required to address those initial five priorities will hit you like a brick the minute you walk in the door. For example, finding out you have an undisclosed lawsuit or that your COO is assaulting your employees—done and done.

Others may be known entities prior to walking in the door. I knew Furr's was a food service business and that it shipped food to a hundred restaurants via its commissary. I also knew that shareholders don't put leadership in place to kill customers, and with one commissary shipping food to one hundred restaurants, we could simultaneously kill people at every one of those one hundred restaurants if we didn't have strong food protections in place. So, within my first week as CEO, I met with our biologist at our FDA-approved facility. Thankfully, this was an area Furr's was getting right. The biologist tested and marked everything that came in and identified what dishes those ingredients were included in and where they were shipped to. This is done so that, say, if a shipment of spinach were found to contain *E. coli*, we would know exactly where that spinach had landed and could get rid of all of it before it became part of a meal (something that happened the following year).

I was also aware, before serving as chair and CEO, that Furr's/ Bishop, Inc. was losing money. Now, it was my job to figure out why. And finally, after serving on the "Board from Hell," I knew there were significant personnel issues. Uncovering those issues would require engaging in another standard practice of mine: Ask your employees questions and then really listen to their responses—you learn a heck of a lot when you do. At the end of the day, the senior staff just want to make you happy so they don't have to share bad news, which means the real issues go unaddressed. Workers in the field, however, have never taken Diplomacy 101 and will answer your questions directly—just make sure you're prepared for the answer.

Right out of the gate, I visited the company's restaurants so I could talk to and listen to the employees in person. On one of those visits, I asked a salad prep employee what she thought was the company's biggest problem. "The CEO," she said, without missing a beat. Now, she had no idea I was the CEO, and I put on what I call my "plastic face," which I employ when I want to remain neutral no matter what is being said.

"Why do you think the CEO is the problem?" I asked.

"The CEO is a banker, not a restaurant person, so they don't know anything about the restaurant business," she replied.

Huh, I thought, *we haven't shared my background with the staff.* Going forward, the employee newsletter included my background, highlighting my extensive restaurant expertise.

The employee's answer was invaluable information—information you can only get directly from the source. Another important component of asking questions is that you cannot punish the people who tell you the truth—ever. And I like to assure people of that with some gesture of thanks for their honesty and helpfulness. One of the best things you can do is show employees that you listened and took action. It was during one such visit that an employee had shared about the COO poking the manager's chest—this kind of news circulates; everyone knew about it. The COO's firing was also circulated by the employees; now they all knew that I listened and took action.

I also listened when Furr's head of HR said to me, "I hate going in and giving a presentation to the board. You all sit there with your calculators, eager to crunch the numbers, and when I start talking about culture, your eyes glaze over."

"OK," I said, pushing aside my HP-12c calculator. "You have my attention. Tell me about culture."

The head of HR explained that the former CEO had sent out an employee survey asking people if they wanted to work over Christmas and be paid overtime or have Christmas off without pay. The resounding response was that the employees didn't care about the pay; they wanted Christmas off. The CEO then proceeded to require employees to work Christmas Day at their regular pay rate.

When he finished explaining, the head of HR looked at me and asked, "What message do you think that sent to our employees?"

"I think I get this culture thing now," I said. "And you just saved me a lot of money. Thank you."

I'd never intentionally considered company culture, having simply operated on my upbringing's principles of treating everyone with dignity and respect. That's how I moved through life, and I expected everyone else to do so as well. Beyond fixing immediate problems, such as the abusive COO, I now realized I needed to consider the broader picture: how the senior team showed up for and conveyed messages to employees, and how the employees viewed their role in the company.

A few months into my new roles, it became apparent that Furr's needed to move its headquarters out of Lubbock (though the restaurant remained in place). We simply did not have the legal and financial support for a public company in Lubbock—all those resources were in Dallas. Moving Furr's out of its founding city was a big deal. And that it was being moved out by a woman, who was a Yankee no less, made it that much more painful.

When I called my friend who was the chief of the Hartford, Connecticut, police and told him about the big announcement I was about to make, he said, "I want you to call the police chief in Lubbock and tell him you're making this announcement."

"You've got to be kidding," I said.

"Put the phone down, Suzanne, go out into the parking lot, and count the number of trucks with gun racks."

When I returned to the phone, I said, "There's a lot of them. OK, I'll call the chief."

"Good idea," he said.

The Lubbock police chief was not surprised by my request. "Tell me when you're going to make the announcement, and I will have police circle around. They'll be out of sight, but nearby."

Alrighty, then, I thought. *This really is a thing*. We also had a senior staff meeting in advance so everyone would be prepared if things went south. Our head of HR, the retired marine, ran the staff meeting. "If there is a problem, your job," he said, pointing to the rest of us, "is to get everybody out so I can focus on taking care of the problem."

By this time, of course, the senior staff had been informed of the move, and for some, it was traumatic. We made offers to everybody, including moving expenses. Some people were excited about the move to Dallas, but of course, for the people who were settled in Lubbock and wanted to stay in Lubbock, I was completely disrupting their lives. I understood that, and thankfully there was no incident around the announcement—but I was glad we had a plan B in place.

The following morning, I went to eat breakfast at one of our restaurants. Back then, everyone read the paper, and on the way to my table, I realized that everyone was looking at my picture at the top of the paper's fold as they read the story of my relocation announcement. *Oh*, I thought, *maybe this is not where I want to have breakfast today*.

One year after I took over as interim CEO, the board found my replacement. And a year after that, once Furr's/Bishop, Inc. was on a steady course and back in good standing, as a board, we began to map out a plan to replace each board member. As chair of the board, my goal was to start an orderly replacement of each board member with a non-workout professional. The crisis had been resolved, and it was now time to fill the seats with a diverse range of business professionals capable of running a now-successful business operation.

My last act was to resign once my replacement was found—an act, I learned afterward, that not enough board members, let alone chairs, take. This is because they don't want to give up the recognition and—depending on the size of the company—their board fee (which may be $1 million per year for large companies).

Unfortunately, board members often hang on long after their value to the organization has expired. I, however, have consistently seen every job as having a beginning and an end. Workout roles are finite—you come in to fix an issue, and once that's done, you go. Fortunately, the entire board understood this because they were all workout professionals, too.

My attorney was astounded: "No one *ever* does that!"

I resisted the urge to say, "Apparently, you don't know enough badasses!"

Chapter 10

From $6 Buffets to Six-Course Meals and Everything in Between

As averse as Frank was to the Furr's $6 all-you-can-eat buffets, he was equally enamored with the six-course meals with wine pairings we dined on at the Castle Hill Inn overlooking Rhode Island's Narragansett Bay … all as part of my job. Between grins of ecstasy, he would say, "This is the best job you've ever had!"

The situation was made even more appealing to him because the thought of me spending $250 per person for a meal was inconceivable. That I was serving on a board of a company that necessitated my dining in such luxury and that they were picking up the tab was hilarious to Frank. I have so many wonderful memories of my time with Newport Harbor Corporation (NHC)—now named Newport Restaurant Group)—memories that reach beyond my love of the cuisine that Frank and I delighted in together.

In 2007, when the owner and chair of NHC, Tim O'Reilly, reached out to me and asked me to consider joining NHC's board, I was filling two requirements for him. One, the board consisted of only men, and Tim wanted to bring women in. Two, he wanted someone with restaurant experience. I checked both boxes. When I joined the board, NHC had been a 100 percent family-owned business for two generations. Tim was the patriarch of both the family and the business, and he had just begun the conversion of the company to an employee stock ownership plan (ESOP), which is an employee benefit plan that enables employees to own 100 percent of the company they work for.

Tim was preparing to retire in the next five or six years and had decided his legacy would be turning NHC over to the employees. Converting to an ESOP requires a tremendous amount of effort, and I admired Tim's willingness to do so. The conversion involves buying out family members who have an ownership in the business (many are often legacy shareholders—family members who had inherited stock in the business over generations), and not all those family members thought this was a wonderful idea. When we were about two-thirds of the way through the process, and the board was a more equal mix of family and nonfamily members, Tim said he was ready to step down and asked me to be chair. I was stunned and so overwhelmed with emotion that I burst into tears. That Tim was placing his beloved family business in my care was the greatest compliment anyone has ever paid me.

When I became chair of NHC in 2013, the CEO, Tim's son Paul, asked me to set up a good old girls' club like he knew I had done at Aetna. I was again stunned. CEOs don't typically want board members hobnobbing with the employees (and with good reason), so we set rules. Our conversations were focused on leadership, and Las Vegas rules applied—nothing we talked about ever left that room. Those lunches were wonderful. The women who attended asked thoughtful questions about my challenges as a leader and how I dealt with them. In following the CEO's goal to develop more women leaders, I offered advice on how the attendees could grow as leaders. I was thrilled to have the opportunity to add this type of value to the organization. And I, of course, learned so much from these women and their shared experiences.

Paul also asked me to visit the company's restaurants and be his eyes and ears. I agreed, with one condition: My picture was never to be in the paper, a newsletter, or anything the employees would see. If I wanted to have a real experience, I needed to go as a guest, not as the board chair. With that agreed, off he sent me to the different restaurants. Sometimes, he'd tell me what he was looking for, and sometimes he wouldn't. Each time, I'd write up a report and send it directly to him, and my job was done. I never shared my comments with the board, because these were operations issues, and operations was the domain of the CEO and the CEO alone.

And who do you think was always my willing dining companion? Frank. He was in seventh heaven anytime an opportunity arose to dine at an NHC establishment. While most of our dining experiences were fantastic, there were occasions when it was hard for me to just sit back and observe and remind myself that I was not there to address issues but merely to report on them. A common practice of mine was to walk around the dining room to see how many people were eating, and in one case, nobody was eating because nobody had been served. I thought, *There's a significant problem in the kitchen.*

As I fumed and fidgeted when it was Frank's and my turn to wait for our meal to be served, Frank said, "I think I might have to strap you to that chair to keep you from going into the kitchen."

"I think you might be right," I replied, "because I want to go in the kitchen right now and ask, 'Are we serving food tonight, or is that not on your agenda?'"

Thankfully, Frank's tackling me was averted when our waiter asked if he could bring us some complimentary oysters from the raw bar, to which Frank happily responded, "Yes! Yes, you can," and I thought, *Nicely done*. That our waiter was paying attention and finding temporary solutions was the good news I shared with Paul. When I shared the extensive wait times, Paul let me know that he was on the verge of firing the executive chef, but he had wanted to hear from me before making the final decision.

"Good idea," I responded.

So many of the observations I shared with Paul were positive. Like the restaurant manager who went up to the hostess and asked, "What needs to be done?" She told him that there was a bunch of tables on the porch that hadn't been cleared and cleaned, and he went directly to the porch and cleared, cleaned, and reset all the tables. Not all restaurant managers see themselves as workers; I could not say enough good things about him.

We visited one of NHC's other restaurants to celebrate my nephew's graduation. We had not mentioned the reason for our visit to the waiter, so we were pleasantly surprised when he brought out a small cake with a candle in it and said with a smile, "I don't know what you're celebrating, but you're clearly celebrating something." That was brilliant. He was clearly paying attention and wanted to go the extra step to make us happy. I couldn't wait to tell the CEO about that.

NHC was an incredible organization to work with, but we still had challenges to navigate. Back in 2000, when I was with Furr's, I had witnessed a shift in the behavior of our customers. One week, Monday might be the busiest night of the week instead of Friday, then the following week it would be Thursday. There seemed to be no way to predict business and, therefore, scheduling. Even though

NHC had a vastly different clientele, Tim had also witnessed this changing dynamic in his customers in 2000. Then, in 2008, we both saw this unpredictable pattern begin to reemerge. I don't know why this type of restaurant behavior is the canary in the coal mine, but it is, so Tim and I advised the board and the company that we needed to take specific steps to prepare for a coming recession. Those steps included taking down cash from our lines of credit, redoing menus to simplify our preparation and lower food costs, reviewing hours of operation and scheduling, and controlling cash flow.

This strategy served us well. The historic market crash occurred in September 2008, catapulting the United States into a deep recession. Banks significantly and swiftly restricted loans, but they were still offering to lend NHC money even while they were shutting off most restaurants. As we stayed the course and rode out the recession, we continued the process of converting to an ESOP.

In an ESOP transition, existing shareholders sell all their shares to an ESOP trust, which holds the shares on the employees' behalf. As I mentioned, when I moved into the role of chair, we had transitioned about two-thirds of the company's shares to the ESOP trust—meaning we had bought out those shares from existing shareholders, who were primarily family members. When only 5 percent of shares are left to be bought out, the company can embark on legal action to take the shares from the last of the non-ESOP shareholders. We were close to having to do that, but fortunately, there were family members willing to reach out to the last holdouts and who convinced them to sell.

After the board meeting that finalized the 100 percent conversion to employee ownership, I walked out to a group of employees who asked, "Did you do it?"

"Yes, we did it," I said with a smile, and then the cheers erupted.

It was a tremendous moment, and I was proud to have been part of it. The employees, while they did not run the company, now had an opportunity to build wealth through their own work, and they had a voice and vote in major decisions such as electing their board of directors. It was funny for me to think that the employees would determine whether I would remain on the board when the next elections came around (I would). The power of it all really hit everyone when, at the end of our first year as an ESOP, a server left with $10,000 in her retirement account. That type of news spreads like wildfire and incentivizes people to commit to their best work and stay with the company, and it continues to be a powerful incentive at what is now Newport Restaurant Group (NRG). The average turnover rate in the restaurant business is 75 percent in a twelve-month period.[8] At NRG in 2019, it was around 14 percent.[9]

I had the pleasure of serving on the board of what was then NHC for over ten years, and I loved every minute of it (and so did Frank!). In October 2018, shortly after Frank's first stroke, I stepped down as chair. I remained as a board member until after Frank's death in 2020, after which, staying on just didn't make sense to me anymore. I did eventually return to the Castle Hill Inn for a delicious six-course meal, but as I sat there overlooking the beautiful Narragansett Bay, sipping my perfectly paired wine, I realized that it had been watching Frank so thoroughly enjoy these moments that had made me happy, and I braced myself for the inevitable wave of grief that followed.

---

8 Stéphanie Mathieu, "Understanding Employee Turnover in the Restaurant Industry," LinkedIn, April 30, 2024, https://www.linkedin.com/pulse/understanding-employee-turnover-restaurant-industry-racmc/.

9 Karen Kahn, "Employee Ownership Drives Success at Newport Restaurant Group," Fifty by Fifty, April 11, 2019, https://www.fiftybyfifty.org/2019/04/employee-ownership-drives-success-at-newport-restaurant-group/.

My foray into restaurant corporations turned out to be an interesting journey; a journey far more enjoyable because Frank had been by my side. While Furr's $6 all-you-can-eat buffet was the beginning and NRG's six-course meals and wine pairings was the ending, in between the two, in the sense of both timeline and cuisine, there was Houlihan's. And, like Furr's, Houlihan's was a brief and bumpy ride.

Chapter 11

With Great Power

On September 11, 2001, I was with my head of franchise development on a flight from Kansas City, Missouri, to Las Vegas, Nevada, to visit a franchise restaurant, when the pilot announced that there had been a national emergency and we would be landing in Albuquerque, New Mexico.

In my decade of frequent flying, I had never heard that one before. *This can't be good,* I thought. I called my head of marketing, because marketing people always know what's going on. This was when calling from a plane cost about a million dollars a minute, but I didn't care. I wanted to know what was happening. He told me that there had been an explosion in New York, and that one of the Twin Towers had collapsed. My first thought was, *He's twenty-eight and has never been to New York—he's probably got that wrong.*

All the other passengers were watching me, waiting for me to share the information I'd just received—like I said, calling from a plane required a small fortune. "There's been an explosion in New York City that has caused some issues," was all I said. I didn't think sharing the additional details that I wasn't sure were accurate was going to help anyone while we were all trapped thirty thousand feet in the air.

Next, I called my COO and told him I wanted every employee who was traveling to be contacted and that he was to speak with each of them to be certain they were safe. Then I called the company's travel agent and told her I needed a car ready for me when we landed in Albuquerque. Everyone would be looking for ground transportation out of Albuquerque, and I didn't want to be left scrambling once we landed. "I don't give a damn if you have to buy the car," I told her.

It was hours before we landed, and I subsequently learned that we were one of the last five planes in the country to land that day and that we had been targeted to be shot down if necessary.

> On the morning of September 11, 2001, nineteen al-Qaeda terrorists hijacked four commercial airplanes. Two of the planes were intentionally flown into the North and South Towers of the World Trade Center in New York City, while a third crashed into the Pentagon in Arlington, Virginia. On the fourth plane, United Airlines Flight 93, passengers learned of the other attacks and fought back, leading to the plane crashing in a vacant field in Western Pennsylvania, around twenty minutes by air from Washington, DC. In total, 2,977 people from ninety countries lost their lives in the attacks.

Once we landed, I told my head of franchise that she was to call her dad, a former Green Beret, to let him know she was OK. Once that was done, we picked up the car and the directions to our headquarters in Kansas City, Missouri, and then we headed to the mall for clothes and charging equipment and got on the road. A couple of hours into our drive, the COO called to let me know that he'd reached everyone except Jim, the deputy head of franchise, who was in DC. Now it was time to reach out to his wife, and I'd be the only one to make that call.

"I can't get a hold of Jim," I told her, trying my best to conceal the dread in my voice.

Fortunately, she had made contact with him. "The battery on his phone is dead," she told me.

I breathed a huge sigh of relief. The whole staff was safe!

By three in the morning, we were only a few hours outside of Kansas City, but we were just too tired to drive any further without rest and pulled into a hotel in Wichita, Kansas. During our drive, staff from the home office had called us every fifteen minutes until one in the morning to check in on us and give us updates, but it wasn't until we watched the news in our hotel that we had our first visual of the devastation of 9/11.

Upon arriving at the home office of Houlihan's Restaurant Group (HRG) the next day, every employee wanted to touch me. It was strange. We held an employee meeting that day, and somebody asked, "We heard that you called the COO and told him to talk to every single person who was traveling. Is that true?"

"Absolutely," I said. "People are the most important part of any organization, and I wanted to know that any of our people who were traveling were safe." That garnered a huge round of applause, and I thought, *Wanting to know your employees are safe is the most obvious thing in the world.* We had franchise restaurants by ground zero; thankfully, all the staff were unharmed.

That same afternoon, I met with the senior staff and asked them what they would have done if they had been in my shoes. Most of them responded that they would have headed for the bar at the Hyatt until they could fly out. This was a good leadership teaching moment on the responsibilities of caring for employees and reassuring them of their safety and the safety of leadership and the organization as a whole.

The next leadership lesson was right out of my father's playbook: "If you are a person of your word, when the shit hits the fan, people will be there for you."

I told my senior staff, "I'm going to call our largest vendors today and tell them that the check is *not* in the mail and ask them to stay with us. If they don't, we may be serving stone soup by the end of today." Making those calls ended up being one of the most hilarious experiences of my life.

The first vendor I called responded, "I've been doing this for twenty-eight years, and I've never had anybody call to tell me the check is *not* in the mail, so let's start with that."

"Well," I said, "as you can imagine, we need to see what our cash position is before we start sending out checks. So as soon as we know that, we'll start doing workout plans with everybody. But right now, I can't send anything out."

"OK. You're going to be honest with me; I'll stay with you."

Next, I called the fish guy and told him no checks would be forthcoming. His first question was, "Where's that accent from?"

"New Hampshire," I replied.

"Your father George McAvoy?" he asked.

I thought, *Are you kidding me? I'm in Kansas City, for God's sake.* "Yes, George McAvoy is my dad."

"Ha! I've been doing business with your father, delivering fish to him, for thirty years. Thank God there's somebody in charge who knows what they're doing. I'll stay with you. I got much bigger problems on the Cape to deal with."

The next vendor responded with, "Can you promise me I won't get hurt?"

"No, I can't," I replied. Bankruptcy law is very clear about what you can and can't say. Here I was asking small businesses to stay with me, even though if Houlihan's ended up in bankruptcy, it could eliminate our debt with them. I didn't offer anything I couldn't deliver.

"OK, now I know you're not going to lie to me. I'll stay with you." And then he asked, "Are you going to the upcoming restaurant conference?"

"Yes, I am."

"Great. I want to meet you." When we met, he said, "I just wanted to meet the person who's going to tell me the truth."

The next vendor said, "We've been following you. You've had a real struggle there that you've been working through for the past year. You've done a fine job and made great progress with Houlihan's. We'll stay with you."

Every call ended with "We'll stay with you." When all the calls were finished, I just sat back and laughed and thought, *Oh my God. I just put in practice what Dad taught me growing up. And it worked!*

The other lesson that came into play with these calls was one I had learned a long time ago: Tell bad news quickly. Bad news is not like a fine wine—it doesn't age well with time. Playing it over and over in your head is not productive; just say it and take whatever punishment follows. I called the senior staff back to share all of this with them.

"So, we're still in business?" they asked.

I said, "We are. We're still going to get food deliveries. I have no idea how we're going to pay for them, but everybody understands we'll figure it out as soon as we can."

When the crisis of September 11, 2001, hit, I had already been serving as CEO of HRG for a year, and oh, what a year it had been.

During the summer of 2000, HRG's sales suddenly went off the cliff. One of the shareholders, watching this disaster, told the chair that they needed to hire somebody to fix this, and that somebody turned out to be me. I was brought in as head of strategy, at which time, nobody knew what that meant, including me.

My first task was to figure out what had gone so drastically wrong. As I visited the restaurants, it became crystal clear to me that Houlihan's had a menu it couldn't deliver on. The current CEO had completely changed the menu and rolled it out to all 150 restaurants simultaneously, without doing any testing in advance. The new menu was heavy on sautéed foods, which overloaded the one-person sauté stations. The domino effect of that logjam was that people were waiting almost two hours to be served their lunch. The HRG clientele were primarily corporate people who were looking for a good but quick lunch. If this situation wasn't fixed fast, sales were going to continue to plummet.

In August 2000, when I reported back to the chair, he knew I was right, and in the blink of an eye, I went from head of strategy to CEO. I subsequently learned that professional, male-led turnaround firms had previously been offered the challenge and had declined, fearing it too risky. *Have no fear*, I thought. *A badass woman is here!*

As the new CEO, a conversation with the CFO was the first thing on my list. In that conversation, I would learn that there had been no bank reconciliations done for over a year—not just for one restaurant but for the entirety of the company. This meant that I had no idea what we had for available cash—and payroll was just two weeks out. I directed the CFO and his team to temporarily hold off on sending out any payments and to call the bank every day and request our bank balance (a practice, I might add, that does not inspire great confidence from your bank). Bank reconciliation, I told the senior staff, was our number one priority. We were running blind and needed to know what our financial position was so we could make the critical decisions that lay before us.

First, we needed to raise some quick cash, and I asked the head of marketing if he had any ideas. His response was that he was working on a strategic plan for one of the board members. My response was that our *only* "strategic plan" was to meet payroll in two weeks. I then called the chair and told him that there can only be one person in charge in a crisis—and that person was me. The offending board member resigned. This is a typical example of a board member not understanding their role or the power it holds.

As a board member, you speak with the volume of a hurricane—employees take every comment far more seriously than intended. Once, at HRG, a board member made an innocuous comment about the parking spaces being tight. The entire garage was relined by the end of the board meeting—I kid you not. That's why I often advise board members: "Just keep your mouth shut!"

With marketing now clear on our immediate strategic direction, we were able to focus on raising capital. The head of marketing suggested coupon drops to bring in fast cash, which it did. Our next priority, almost parallel to making payroll, was fixing the menu so we could deliver good food in a timely manner. I had the test kitchen give me five or six items that could be delivered within fifteen minutes. We tested those items out in five restaurants and then rolled them out to all 150 with a marketing campaign announcing that our new lunch menu could be delivered within just fifteen minutes. This would resolve the "It's going to take me two hours to have lunch at Houlihan's" mindset and stop the financial bleeding. Once people started coming back, we began working on a revamped menu that went through a thorough process with the test kitchen and then a gradual rollout to all the restaurants.

I loved working with the team in the test kitchen, even though I was never allowed to have any input in the tasting (they knew I had a stone palate). My input was hammering home the number of steps it took for any dish to go from order to delivery while maintaining consistent quality no matter which restaurant was serving it. Houlihan's key lime pie, which at some restaurants was like jelly and at others immovable, required fifteen steps. "Too many steps," I told the kitchen. "Either limit the steps and make it easy for every restaurant to replicate consistently, or take it off the menu."

By the spring of 2001, our cash flow had stabilized, and while we still sat on the edge of crisis mode (oblivious to the real crisis awaiting us just a few months ahead on September 11), we were now able to develop our sustainability efforts. One of those efforts was the implementation of a path of progression for every employee.

It was important to me that we committed to our employees in this way. A few years earlier, I said to my team of eight at The Hopgood Group, "If I get hit by a truck tomorrow, you're out of a job. So, we are going to talk about how you would be prepared for that so you have options." I never wanted people to be left in the lurch because of something I'd done (even if it was unintentionally getting hit by a truck).

At HRG, the case was more compelling, because leadership had so blatantly failed its employees, and so we needed to regain their respect and trust. The decision to introduce a brand-new menu to all 150 locations without testing it first had resulted in the company's sales plummeting, and when that happened, so did the tips that so many of the staff depended on for their livelihood. Because of that income insecurity, theft was rampant. Tip adjusting was one such method of theft. The server would take a receipt and round up certain numbers; for example, changing a five or a three to an eight. If you were on a corporate account, would you really notice if your credit card statement had $38 rather than the $33 or $35 you spent? Likely not. Then there was the "$1 for Houlihan's, $1 for me" practice with cash transactions, which occurred mostly at the bar—when I ordered an audit at our largest restaurant operation, our receipts were $10,000 higher for the bar than they had been the previous week. In this case, it was because a bartender was doing the $1-for-$1 cash split.

There was also rampant food theft. I once asked a psychologist why this occurs, and she explained that when someone sees their fellow employees taking a steak or a chicken or whatever for dinner and nothing happens to them, that person begins to think themselves the fool and convinces themselves that taking food is part of their compensation. And at some point, if that person is the only holdout when it comes to stealing, they become a risk to the other employees and will therefore be pressured to steal as well. That pressure can be hard to resist, especially if you are no longer making enough money to live on. I also found IOUs in the company's safe from employees long gone, for money they had "borrowed."

During this time, some on the leadership team continued to accept gifts and favors—this does not build the right culture when your employees are turning to theft to make ends meet. When I learned that the head of purchasing went to the Masters Tournament every year, compliments of our largest food vendor, I appointed the COO as head of ethics for Houlihan's. Anyone considering accepting a gift had to run the gift by him. I also told the staff that, as CEO, I would not accept gifts, and I instructed my secretary to return any gift sent to me with a note saying how much I would appreciate a gift but that I had a policy of not accepting any. The values I had fought so hard to maintain at Aetna had not changed, and I told my staff that there was only one reason people would be giving me anything, and that was to buy favor—something I would not partake in. What I didn't share was the reason I didn't want to know what any of the gifts were—it would be painful to reject a gift such as tickets to the Super Bowl on the fifty-yard line! Not knowing what I was giving up seemed like an obvious move.

Once customers returned and sales (and tips) picked up again, we were able to put the path to progression into practice. It was a much heavier lift with six thousand employees than it had been with my team of eight at The Hopgood Group, but with HRG, I had a team of supervisors and a full HR department with a highly competent HR director to implement the program.

The HR director that was in place had been with Houlihan's for many years when the beloved CEO Fred Hipp left the company. Shortly after the new CEO (the one responsible for the menu debacle) and his team took over, that HR head and many others left the organization. When I arrived, the HR person in place was beyond unprofessional, and I couldn't wait to get rid of her. The staff that had remained after Fred's departure praised the former HR head, and so I pursued her. She agreed to meet me for dinner (at a non-Houlihan's restaurant), and I was determined to persuade her to come back before our meal was over. As we were finishing our entrée, it was getting late. I informed the owner that I was not leaving his restaurant until I had convinced this woman to return to Houlihan's, so if we needed to run past closing, he needed to let me know what I had to do to allow us to remain.

Fortunately, just as our desserts were being placed in front of us, this beloved HR professional agreed to return to her position as head of HR. With her at the helm, our plan for a path to progression was well implemented.

Every supervisor was required to sit down with each of their direct reports and walk them through the steps to the next level they wanted to attain. Whether that was education, applying for a different position, or skills training, we needed to help them map out those steps and support them in reaching them. I wanted our employees to know that we cared about them. Shortly after our plan was implemented, people came up to me, thanking me for thinking of them and their future. I wasn't able to witness the full benefits of this program because, when 9/11 hit just a few months later, we returned to crisis mode, and this time, we were unable to recover. That's when I found myself on the receiving end of a workout.

Chapter 12

The Right Thing to Do

"Would you mind changing offices?"

"Excuse me?" I replied. I had heard their question; I just couldn't believe they had asked it.

"Would you mind changing offices?" they asked again.

Immediately following the attack of 9/11, HRG's sales dropped 25 percent. We tried to recover, and as I shared in the last chapter, our vendors had agreed to work with us on good faith. But we had not fully stabilized from the first time our sales went off the cliff the previous year, so we simply didn't have the means to recover quickly enough. It wasn't long before the lenders that held our mortgage took over. Once the workout team arrived for the takeover, I fully expected to be booted out the door the same day—a practice I had employed with every takeover I was involved in.

That, however, is not how this workout worked out. Rather than showing me the door, the workout team asked if I would mind changing offices. Once I realized their question was sincere, I replied, "Not at all." I moved into my new office, and they kept me on for a few months in what I can only describe as an advisory role. This was remarkable to me because, as you now know, when I am the lead workout person in a takeover, I go in and immediately ask for the keys and the combination to the safe and then politely show management the door.

The workout team asked me to attend some meetings and offer insights that they wouldn't necessarily have access to. They also asked me to speak to the employees and explain to them that this bankruptcy process was a good thing for Houlihan's. I didn't think it was, and I knew, as did the workout team, that the employees would follow my lead. Since the bank had not negated my contract (which is usually what happens in bankruptcy), I was still obligated to fulfill it. So, I called my good friend who helps me work through these sorts of things, Mike Tankersley.

"Mike," I said, "I don't think I can do this because I don't think this bankruptcy is a good thing."

To which he replied, "Shut your door, get a pen and paper, and I'm going to dictate what you're going to say." And he did, and of course, everything he said was true. "The banks are taking over Houlihan's, and that's good, because they have money. That means we don't have to worry about liquidity issues anymore. With the bank's funding, we will be able to continue operating the business so you can all continue working. This is a good thing." I couldn't have come up with that on my own, but it was the right thing to do, and Mike was always all about the right thing to do. He had made that clear in our first conversation in 1998 when I was chair at Furr's, and we chose Mike's firm—over the one whose counsel mistook me for the coffee girl—as outside counsel.

Right out of the gate, Mike had made it clear that any advice he gave me would not just be legal; it would also be the right thing to do. "Giving only legal advice," he told me, "is the lowest possible bar for a lawyer. If that's what you are looking for, we'll work on finding you someone else, because my advice will never be the lowest bar."

"I'm not interested in the lowest bar," I assured him.

I had never run a public company before. I had never run a restaurant company with thousands of employees before. So, Mike had been a brilliant choice for me, not only for his legal prowess but for what would turn into a lifelong friendship. Mike is one of those friends, like Rachel Roginsky, who believes (and makes me believe) that I can do things I've never done before. In the situation I found myself in at HRG, Mike was like my one lifeline call to a friend. I spoke the words he had dictated to me and assured the employees that the banks would get Houlihan's back on its feet, and they did. In fact, the workout team completed the bankruptcy process in record time. The speed and efficiency with which this was done were due, in large part, to my team and I already having prepared a bankruptcy plan for one of HRG's restaurant chains, called Darryl's.

Darryl's had been another piece of the puzzle I discovered when I came up for air from the Houlihan's menu catastrophe. This chain of fifteen restaurants that HRG owned was killing us, and the only way we could mitigate Darryl's before it took down all of HRG was to get out of the leases for all its locations. The landlord for the leases refused to entertain any lease negotiations, forcing me to pull out the big guns. I would need to threaten bankruptcy if he didn't release us from our leasing contract. I don't like to bluff, so before I made that threat, I wanted to have a bankruptcy plan ready to send the landlord to show that we were prepared to go to court to eliminate the leasing contracts, which would leave them with nothing. The hope was that they would prefer to have something and so would be willing to negotiate a deal. But before we could formally make the threat, 9/11 happened, and the Houlihan's restaurants were also at risk.

Our advanced planning had positioned the banks well as they proceeded with their bankruptcy filing. They smartly leveraged my knowledge and the employees' allegiance to me by keeping me involved in the initial process. And when they did finally (and nicely) show me the door, they shipped all my belongings from my condo back home to Hartford—something they did not have to do. I truly enjoyed working with the people at HRG and was heartbroken when we couldn't turn it around.

My experience with Furr's and HRG shifted my focus for The Hopgood Group from hotel consulting to workouts. It was an interesting transition. When I was at Furr's, I had told my small staff of eight at The Hopgood Group that while I wasn't going to let anyone go, they all needed to find other jobs. With workouts, I had access to the employees of the company I was doing the workout for, so I didn't need any employees of my own.

Furr's and HRG taught me that running a company with thousands of employees is easier than running a business with a handful of people. When you are CEO of a group of eight, you are also the CFO, COO, and head of HR, and just like I didn't have the personality to be a teacher or a nurse, I was not well-suited for HR. I am not that person who has the patience to listen to employees complain about what their coworkers said and how it made them feel—I'm just not. My response in that situation would likely be, "Can we please get back to work?" The transition was a good move, and as knowledge spread of my expertise working with companies in crisis and of my reputation for making my voice heard and standing my ground when it came to making the tough decisions (i.e., my badassery), I was offered opportunities to serve on a variety of boards and committees. You can probably guess by now that I'm rarely asked to take on a board position because everything is going swimmingly.

In 2003, I became chair of my first NASDAQ company. This was a position that led me to always ask myself, "When I take a good look at the people on the board, are they people I want to be in a deposition with?" before I said yes to a new board position. It's a valid question (and one I frequently encourage others to ask themselves) because you simply do not know what you do not know about the company. And the bit you do not know may result in the CEO calling to let you know that he is walking into federal court to enter a guilty plea for defrauding the Department of Defense (DOD).

Months prior to that chilling call from the CEO, the board had received notice from the DOD that basically told us we were in big trouble. Here's the bit that neither I nor anyone on the board had known: Although the company was certifying that every single piece we manufactured was built to military specifications, the truth was that the company had omitted a step in the manufacturing process. The CEO, who was an engineer, assured the board that the omitted step was meaningless.

"That argument doesn't matter," I said. "We signed a document that said for every single part we made, we followed military specs, and we didn't. And," I continued, "we knowingly didn't. That is fraud."

"Well," the CEO repeated, "that last step that we didn't do wasn't necessary."

"That's not the point," I reiterated. "And please tell me that the step we didn't take will not put anyone at risk." This was a pertinent question because the parts we were manufacturing were being installed in fighter jets.

"No," he said, "I told you that step didn't matter."

"Again, not the point," I said. "When you are legally signing off that you did in fact take that step—it had better be true."

Every single component of every piece of equipment we made and signed off on carried an individual penalty. We had made thousands of the component in question, resulting in a costly fine. We had to sell a division of the company to pay for the CEO's illegal actions.

Immediately after receiving that first notice from the DOD, I visited the offices of the other divisions and discovered more bits the board did not know. I was told by the division leaders that they had been directed to hold off on paying bills because the company was having cash flow issues. This was a drastically different financial picture than the one the CEO had been feeding us. Lying is a line in the sand for me. I cannot work with someone who lies to me, and once again, I found myself on the phone with Mike Tankersley.

"Mike," I said, after explaining our situation, "I cannot work with a CEO who isn't straight with me. I just can't. Please tell me I can resign as chair."

"Legally, you can," said Mike. "But the right answer is no, you can't. Being chair of a company is a critical job, Suzanne, and you have a fiduciary duty to find a competent replacement before you resign."

"Mike," I said, "I'm going to press the buzzer, and we're going to start this conversation again. And just so you know, when we do, I'm looking for a different answer from you because I really, really want to resign from this board."

Of course, Mike insisted on repeating the right thing to do. It was agony, but six months later, my very competent replacement was in place, and I was able to resign in the spring of 2005.

After I left, I served as an expert witness for a couple of years. It's a good gig. Ninety percent of it is research, which equates to a lot of reading—reading you can do anywhere. I would receive boxes and boxes of documents that I would read on the plane, at the beach, wherever I wanted, and I would bill ridiculous amounts of money for doing so. They were, of course, paying for my expertise (not my reading skills), which was extensive. I had an ability to see all the pieces to the puzzle and how they all fit together in ways others could not, which often led to me solving the case for the attorneys of record.

I remember one case in which I cracked the code for missing deferred income pension funds. I explained to the litigators that the actions taken by senior staff to access their pension funds were because the company had been trying, unsuccessfully, for years to refinance its debt before it came due. As a result, senior staff were concerned that the company would have to file for bankruptcy, and in a bankruptcy, deferred compensation accounts become an asset of the corporation. There is a ninety-day lookback period in bankruptcy (a period during which past financial activity is examined for irregularities), so the approval and withdrawal of funds had to be executed before the debt became due. All the parties approving the action were duped into believing they were doing something different. Here's the why, when, and how this all played out.

The chair of the compensation committee was given a document by the organization's general counsel and simply told that what he was being asked to sign provided the employees with an option for certain actions. What they didn't specify was that one of those actions was withdrawing their deferred compensation funds, which is what the chair really approved, and it led to the employees withdrawing all their funds. The chair followed protocol in signing on the advice of the general counsel without reading the document (as that is what the general counsel is paid to do). Because the timing was so strange, I was curious, and I began to dig deeper. When I pieced together the company's ongoing attempts to refinance its $500 million debt through the lens of a ninety-day bankruptcy lookback, I understood why the withdrawals had happened ninety days prior to the debt coming due and a potential bankruptcy filing. Only because I knew bankruptcy law was I able to figure out the actions and the timing and resolve the questions of why, when, and how.

Of course, as an expert witness, there is the unfortunate element of being deposed or taking the witness stand in court and fighting against an opposing counsel who has spent a whole career and a great deal of time and money trying to discredit expert witnesses. That part was not so fun and relied on my knowing all the facts and being able to present them.

I was recently asked if I would serve as an expert witness. My first thought was, *Yes, that could be fun.* My next thought was, *Wait a minute. To be an expert witness, I have to be current on all things related to the expertise required. Do I really want to start attending meetings and conferences to keep up to date?* I quickly realized the answer to that question was no. As tempting as it was, I was thoroughly enjoying my retirement and the limited responsibilities I now had.

My expert witness roles further established the depth of my expertise and my commitment to getting to the truth, and I was asked more and more to join boards and committees. In 2007, those opportunities were at an all-time high. It was the year that kicked off my incredible run with the NHC. Spring of that same year, I joined Point Blank Solutions (formerly DHB Industries) as director and chair of nominating/governance, and then I rounded out the year with my new role as managing director of board advisory services with the NACD. Of the three, Point Blank would prove to be my shortest run and my most dramatic exit.

Point Blank was the sole provider of bullet-resistant vests for US soldiers in Iraq. The chair of the board was a retired four-star general, and the board was made up of law enforcement and military men who had never worked with a woman at their level. This was all new territory for them, and I knew I just had to wait out the awkwardness while they figured out how and if they could work with me. Honestly, I just wanted them to stop hopping up and running to open doors for me every time I walked into and out of a room—it was exhausting. But I knew nothing I did was going to change until they were ready and that, sooner or later, somebody was going to get tired of all the dancing around and test me to see if I had a sense of humor and if they could have an open exchange with me. It was the retired commissioner of the California Highway Patrol who finally administered my "test."

In the middle of a board meeting, he asked, "What's in your pocketbook, Suzanne?"

Everybody exchanged uncomfortable looks around the table. Without hesitation, I put my pocketbook on the table, opened it, and proceeded to dump its contents out.

"You don't carry much," he said, looking at my small assortment of keys, wallet, lipstick, pen, and small notebook.

"I carry what I need," I replied.

Everybody looked at the commissioner, and then they all started laughing. Once I had shown them that my feathers weren't easily ruffled and that I had a sense of humor, I could almost hear their collective sigh of relief that I "fit" their company culture. They began kidding with me in the same way they did with each other, and we finally got down to business.

I landed on this board of military and law-enforcement men because Point Blank's chair—retired four-star General Ellis, who was a highly competent operations guy—did not have any public company or SEC board experience, let alone for a company that manufactured a life-or-death product for the DOD. That type of business requires a board with knowledge of and expertise in companies in crisis. In his search for board members with the right skill sets, General Ellis came across a book that Mike Tankersley and I had coauthored in 2005, *Board Leadership for the Company in Crisis*[10], and he determined I had the skill set he needed for Point Blank's board.

When General Ellis asked me to serve on the board, I was surprised, but I heard his confidence in choosing me for this role, and I chose to listen. "Yes, sir," was my reply.

Our job as a board was to handle all the investigations—think SEC, IRS, FBI, and CIA—so that operations could focus on manufacturing the bulletproof vest without any extraneous distractions. These were difficult issues to address, issues that required open and honest dialogue, which occasionally meant pushing back on the general. It didn't take long for me to realize that my fellow board members were disinclined to tell the general he was wrong. I remember one instance when we had to file publicly that Point Blank was involved in SEC investigations. General Ellis wanted to adjust our messaging. The changes he was suggesting were a bad idea and possibly not SEC-compliant.

Outside of the board meeting, a fellow board member suggested I might best be suited to tell the general he was wrong. While I was probably the most knowledgeable in relation to the SEC, the more pressing reason I was being nominated to share the bad news was because the other board members were all former military, and the idea of telling a general that they disagreed with him was inconceivable. Never one to shy away from telling people when they're right or wrong, I shared the board's concerns with General Ellis. As it turned out, he was greatly relieved to know that someone on the board would do the right thing and tell him when he was making a decision that was bad for the company.

10 Suzanne Hopgood and Michael W. Tankersley, *Board Leadership for the Company in Crisis* (National Association of Corporate Directors, 2005).

One of those SEC investigations was a result of the founder of Point Blank being indicted for wiring public company money to Senegal, where we didn't have an extradition treaty, for which he was sentenced to seventeen years in prison.

At the time of his indictments (a whopping 122 counts), the founder owned 45 percent of the company's stock. He was subsequently approached by a private equity firm that was looking to take control of the company, and this equity firm proposed its own slate of board members to execute the takeover strategy. I was serving as chair of the governance committee at the time, which meant I would be involved in vetting and recommending all potential candidates, and I would need to do so with impartiality. Impartiality was the key word here, and something I did not think I could achieve while still serving as chair of the governance committee, so I removed myself as a candidate for reelection. The board disagreed with that strategy, but I knew it was the right thing to do, and I stuck to my guns.

We appealed to the Delaware court, where the company was registered, to not allow the founder to vote with his 45 percent of the company's shares since he was under indictment, but the founder prevailed. The private equity firm won the proxy contest, and we were all ousted in one fell swoop.

The culture among Point Blank's board of directors was like no other I had experienced before. I knew from that onset that I needed to listen to who its members were and how they worked, all while allowing them the time to understand if and how I fit. With a little time and a collective sigh of relief, I was accepted by this remarkable group of men, who, with their clear focus on the company, had achieved great success. I was sorry when it all came to an end.

Chapter 13

We're Not in Kansas Anymore

It was at the end of 2007, while I was still knee-deep in Point Blank Solutions and still working as an expert witness, that I accepted the role of managing director of board advisory services for the NACD. You may recall that this is the position that enabled Frank and me to travel the world. Roger Raber, then–executive director of the NACD, had recruited me to give presentations on corporate governance at the association's annual meeting and as a paid speaker for the corporate training sessions the NACD conducted at client board meetings.

The work I did for the NACD, first in my role as a speaker and then as the head of the NACD corporate governance Board Advisory Services, solidified me as a national expert in corporate governance and risk. It also solidified my understanding of the importance of appreciating and respecting the various cultures I would find myself working in, whether that was in another state or on the other side of the globe.

One of the funniest examples of this necessitated Mike's assistance—this time, in person. I was scheduled to present to a corporate board in Denver, and in preparation, I looked up the board members.

Every board member represented one of the biggest oil and gas companies in the country. That gave me pause. As a woman *and* a Yankee, I thought I might not be the best choice for this presentation. I made a call to the NACD and asked if Mike (also an NACD member and a Texan) could join me. As I could have predicted, Mike walked in, and they all looked down at his cowboy boots. I could almost hear their collective, "Yep, we're good."

Within seconds, they had all started talking about whom they knew in Texas. "Sure, I know so-and-so. I ride the elevator with them every day in Dallas," or "I just had a couple of beers with …" All these shared familiarities would be followed with a nod of recognition. Mike brought me the credibility that I needed to get the oil executives to take me seriously. When they saw I was with him, I was good to go.

When the presentation was over, I said to Mike, "You know, you do a great good ol' boy impression."

"I am a good ol' boy," he said. "I do a really good impression of a corporate lawyer."

My work at Furr's in Texas had been my first introduction to the importance of understanding the culture I was working in and that, to understand it, I must listen to the advice of others who knew better than me. Like when the Hartford police chief advised me to count the gun racks on the pickup trucks that sat in the Furr's parking lot and then call the local police chief for guidance before making my relocation of Furr's from Lubbock to Dallas announcement.

Or when Mike's guidance saved me from making a huge mistake when I tried to resolve the outrageous cost of the workers' compensation claims of Furr's. It was while on a visit to the commissary that I saw firsthand the reason for our high slip-and-fall rate: All the truck drivers were wearing cowboy boots. *Of course*, I thought, *they were all slipping on the smooth concrete floors.* My immediate and logical business solution was that we would institute a new footwear policy that mandated rubber-soled shoes.

When I shared my findings and proposed solution with Mike, he gently said, "Don't you have other priorities to address before you try to solve this one?"

OK, I thought, *there was a message there. Got it. Let's leave this one alone for the moment and let me think about it a little more.* I learned, over time, that when Mike nicely suggested I had other priorities, what he meant in New England terms was, "That's a dumbass idea, Suzanne." In hindsight, when I think of Furr's slip-and-fall problem, I can clearly see the mutiny that would have taken place if I had acted on my own instincts and banned something as important to their culture as cowboy boots—and rightly so.

It became a funny story to tell at board presentations. I could just feel the audiences' concern for my safety when I told them how I had planned on dealing with the issue: "Oh, that poor woman from Connecticut." At one presentation, someone asked if I was going to recommend that the Texas truck drivers wear Birkenstocks instead. That got a big laugh.

At one in-boardroom presentation, I was awed by the culture of caring in the remote area of Utqiagvik (formerly known as Barrow), Alaska, which sits at the northernmost point of the United States, well north of the Arctic Circle. The residents of the region were inextricably linked to nature and each other. Ten-foot whaling boats would motor out in search of whales. When they returned with a sixty-ton whale in tow, the entire village had a job in dismantling the whale for its many purposes, including food, fuel, and materials for crafts and trade. It was fascinating to observe. Wild animals were only killed for food and were always sectioned up for the population. By tradition, the first food excised from the whale went to the elderly. Theirs was a culture of people who took care of each other, and it was clear that the well-being of the community's people would need to sit at the center of any corporate board governance and determine the risks they were willing to take.

When giving presentations in Hong Kong, Moscow (twice), São Paulo, and Rio de Janeiro, it was important to understand the varying cultures and how to most respectfully give my presentation considering that English was not my audiences' first language. I learned to speak slowly, in short, declarative sentences, and was frequently rewarded for my efforts when I saw people begin to remove their simultaneous translation headsets. In Moscow, boards were trying to learn the rules so they could list on the NYSE. Understanding their objectives and regulations was critical, though sometimes, cultural differences were best left unaddressed. In one such situation, a gentleman had asked what numbers we used when reporting financials.

"Well, we only have one set of numbers," I said cautiously.

"Oh," he said, "if we disclosed our real financials, we'd have to pay taxes." I quickly moved the conversation to a new topic.

I would carry that appreciation of cultural knowledge and understanding into the work I did in my own backyard of Hartford. That work would occur in both my role as chair of the NRG and my role as chair of Hartford's Capital Region Development Authority (CRDA). I served as the governor-appointed chair for the CRDA for ten truly wonderful years, and in that time, we only had one significant upheaval within the board related to housing in the city. Specifically, the converting of a vacant office building into studio apartments. There were several board members adamant that we should not move forward with the project because they "didn't know anyone who would want to live in a four-hundred-square-foot studio apartment."

Well, of course they didn't, because they couldn't imagine the thought of living in that small a space. It was a fascinating and heated discussion, and fortunately, one we were able to move forward from. Young people today live entirely differently than we did. The building now has a movie theater, an extensive fitness center, a rooftop lounge, and common area rooms on each floor (a yoga studio, library, conference room, etc.). Young people live in small spaces and use the common area spaces to gather (no dinner parties for this group!). It's a sea change from when we were growing up. We moved ahead with the conversion of the office building into five hundred studio apartments. Within three months, 90 percent of them were leased. During my time with the CRDA, we converted vacant office buildings around the city into three thousand apartments that have consistently maintained a 92 percent occupancy rate—one of the highest in the nation. I am one of those occupants, and yes, you can bet I was happy to invite the naysayers over and say, "Look who's living in a four-hundred-square-foot apartment in downtown Hartford!"

As that debate at the CRDA was playing out in 2015, I could foresee the same thing happening at NRG. Our customer base was primarily baby boomers, and well, like everything else, we boomers have a shelf life, and we aren't going to be around forever to enjoy expensive six-course meals. We needed to think about the future, and so our CEO, Paul, began working on new restaurant concepts. Before he could roll his ideas out to our (primarily boomer) board, I shared with him what I had just experienced with the older wealthy suburbanites at the CRDA.

"Let's do some field testing with the board before we open up the discussion about your new concepts," I suggested, and he agreed.

So, on a Monday night, Paul and I gathered the board and headed out on a field trip to West Hartford. When we got settled and were reading the menu at dinner, one board member said, "Look around—the restaurant is full of people eating, and those people are significantly younger than us."

The person next to him stated, "I don't see anything on this menu that I can eat."

And I thought to myself, *Therein lies the meeting that I'm trying to avoid, because you are not the subject of what we're trying to do.* I said nothing.

The next morning when the CEO arrived for breakfast in the hotel restaurant, he said, "That was a lot of food. When I went to bed, my body said I needed to stay vertical for a bit to give it time to digest."

When the COO arrived, he said, "I've never eaten so much in one sitting in my life."

I thought those were two good messages about love of the food, especially from the COO, who was NRG's former executive chef. Over the next couple of days, we did a tour of restaurants with young clientele in West Hartford. They were different from NRG's current restaurants, but they were all good and packed full. I was proud that, after leaving the heated CRDA meeting, I could foresee the same culturally biased arguments happening at NRG and was able to get ahead of them.

As the NRG board moved forward on developing our new restaurant concepts, there wasn't even a peep of "No one's going to eat there ..." because we had already seen the proof that they were.

I spent ten years as the chair of the CRDA, and when I decided it was time for me to step down, I was asked to reconsider. Yes, we were still doing good work under my leadership, and yes, I could still bring value to the work, but that didn't mean I was still the best person for the job. The world changes quickly, and it's critical that new ideas, perspectives, and leadership are continually engaged to meet those changes in the best way possible. To make way for new leaders—and yes, that includes younger people who have differing visions for the future and the knowledge to get us there—those of us currently leading must recognize when it's our time to exit.

But before my departure from the CRDA, I would navigate what would be two of the most difficult and, in many ways, richest years of my life.

Chapter 14

To the Moon and Back

On the morning of September 25, 2018, I headed out to run errands and then meet Frank at the gym. When Frank didn't arrive, I gave him a call to see where he was.

"I'm having some trouble navigating," he said.

"I'm on my way," I told him, ending the call and heading for the door.

When I walked in, Frank was still in bed. "I can't get up," he said.

Alarm bells sounded in my head, "OK," I said, as calmly as I could. "Let's get you dressed and get out of here."

To this day, I cannot come up with a rational explanation of why I thought it was necessary for him to get dressed—did I think they wouldn't let him into the ER in his jammies? Also, why was I not calling an ambulance?

I started grabbing clothes and helping Frank change while he sat on the edge of the bed, trying to keep his balance. Once dressed, my five feet two frame helped his six foot four frame stand up. Being so much shorter, it made it easy for Frank to lean on me like a cane.

As we made our way out the door, I talked him through every step we were taking, "OK, we're going to walk to the elevator," "We're going to walk to the door," and, once I helped Frank prop himself against the outside wall of the building, "Stay right here. I'm going to bring the car around."

When we arrived at the hospital, I pulled into the ambulance entrance and hopped out of the car, yelling "I need help!" Staff came running with a wheelchair, and they took Frank right into an exam room where they peppered us with questions before whisking him off for a CAT scan that would uncover a significant brain bleed. With the results back, the questions resumed, and once the staff realized that Frank had already taken his morning *and* evening blood thinners (when I arrived home, I noticed that he had double-dosed himself), they scrambled to reverse the blood thinner because that was the last thing in the world they wanted pumping through his system while his brain was bleeding.

The medical system does not speak English that I can understand. So at this point, while I was able to take in bits and pieces, I was not fully understanding what those bits and pieces actually meant.

Thankfully, our friend Dr. Bob Painter met me at the ER and served as a translator. With each new doctor, Dr. Bob was also able to assure me of their competence for taking good care of Frank.

When the doctor first came in to see Frank in the ER, he asked who I was.

"I'm the spouse," I replied.

Then he asked who Dr. Bob was. "I'm Dr. Painter."

"And your specialty?" asked the ER doctor.

"Cardiovascular surgery," Dr. Bob said, and then he assured the ER doctor that he was not there to second-guess but to be a support for me.

When Frank was moved to the ICU, we were introduced to Dr. Pervez.

When I introduced Dr. Bob, he told Dr. Pervez, "My only purpose here is to keep Suzanne sane."

To which Dr. Pervez replied, "Well, you're not doing a very good job," which gave us all a much-needed laugh.

It wasn't until after Dr. Pervez left and Dr. Bob said the words "Frank had a stroke" that it finally registered. The right side of Frank's face drooped, and he couldn't move his right arm, so everyone assumed I knew what had happened, but I hadn't made the connection until that moment.

Between his stay in the hospital and rehab, Frank wouldn't return home until March 1, 2019. The rehab facility was not a good environment for Frank. Even though it was the best one I could find, its physical setup often left the patients isolated from staff and other patients. Apart from his daily hour of physical therapy (PT) to try to regain some balance and strength, Frank was left alone in his room with the TV on. We are not TV viewers. I spent every day with Frank while he was in rehab, wheeling him around and seeking out interactions. Frank's new workout guy—Steve, a retired police officer—and I managed to sneak Frank out one night to attend a hockey game.

Bringing Frank home was the best thing for him, and I wish I had brought him home sooner, but I just didn't know what the right thing to do was. Frank's physical and cognitive abilities were still severely affected, but it was clear that he was with us and understood what was happening around him.

As I contemplated Frank coming home, I asked my friend Kathy, who is an advanced practice registered nurse, if she thought I could take care of Frank myself. She looked at me as if I'd lost my mind. She then quickly dispelled any delusions I had that Frank would progress enough in rehab that he would require only minimal help at home. Frank would be coming home in a wheelchair, unable to stand or transfer in and out of that chair without assistance. We ordered a hospital bed for the house and then, with Kathy's assistance, began interviewing full-time caregivers.

Some of the potential caregivers never even spoke to Frank during the interview—it took everything I had not to just tell them to leave. Then Leroy arrived. Leroy *saw* Frank; he spoke *to* Frank, and when the rehab aide came to bring Frank to PT, Leroy asked if he could go too so that he could learn what they did and how it was done.

Frank's first night home, Frank, Steve, and I went to a Fleetwood Mac concert at the XL Center, which was just two blocks from our home. Living in downtown Hartford, in what we came to call the "six-block wheelchair radius," played a significant role in allowing Frank and me to keep living our lives. We continued to be frequent attendees at the XL Center, going to entertainment events and hockey games. The Bushnell Center for the Performing Arts, TheaterWorks, Real Art Ways, and the Stage Company were other venues we frequented. Our favorite place to meet up with friends for breakfast, Ashley's Restaurant, was also within that six-block radius. Leroy was our constant companion, navigating Frank and his wheelchair through the city—or, if we were heading to Dillon Stadium (now known as Trinity Health Stadium) for a soccer game, transferring Frank in and out of the car. We became a trio of sorts, enjoying the active social life that the city had to offer.

Leroy was a true gift to us. He not only took great care of Frank, but he did it with such joy. Leroy would frequently sing and dance for Frank, and there was one night when Frank was able to join in. Leroy is Jamaican, so of course the three of us went to Dillon Stadium the night the Jamaican soccer team was playing. During halftime, there was a Jamaican band performing, and Leroy, with a huge smile on his face, danced in step with the band's lead singer while spinning Frank around in his wheelchair to the music. It was pure magic to see Frank having so much fun. Being able to surround Frank with as much joy and laughter as possible gave me a chance to show him how much I loved him. That was very important to me.

In October 2019, Leroy hurt his shoulder, and although he (and his wife) remained in our lives, he was no longer able to be Frank's caregiver. We tried a couple of other caregivers that the agency sent over, but they did not work out. One of the caregivers did not speak English and once tried to get Frank to stand up by just repeating his unintelligible command to Frank louder and louder. Frank could *hear* what the caregiver was saying and really wanted to fulfill the request but did not understand what he was trying to convey. This so frustrated Frank that he yelled "Fuck you!" In our almost forty years together, I had never heard Frank speak those words until that moment. That caretaker became known to Team Frank as "F you, John," which made us all laugh every time we talked about him.

When the agency sent Dwayne to us for an interview as a potential replacement for "F you, John," we felt like we had been given another gift. Dwayne, like Leroy, was incredibly kind and caring, and he too became an integral part of our lives. I honestly do not know how we would have not only survived but managed to thrive through this stage in our life without the two of them. Leroy and Dwayne made it possible for me to remain Frank's loving companion rather than his daily caregiver—and that is a gift for which there are no words.

By the time Dwayne came into our world, Frank had made great strides cognitively. But that improvement was a double-edged sword. While I was thrilled to see Frank's personality shine more brightly, I was concerned that his increased cognition would also mean he would be aware that he was not going to recover. Because of the risk of a brain bleed, Frank was no longer taking blood thinners, and because he was no longer taking his blood thinners, he was frequently throwing clots (having strokes). This was not survivable.

Frank and I were so lucky to be surrounded by so many wonderful friends and sources of support. Team Frank included Leroy and his wife, Doreen; Dwayne; Frank's wonderful workout partner, Steve; his caring physical therapist, Tracey; and, of course, Kathy and Dr. Bob—all of whom played a crucial role in the many wonderful moments of Frank's last two years with us.

Because of all the love and support, Frank and I were able to continue enjoying life as fully as possible while honoring his wishes. Frank and I had determined years before what we did *not* want to happen in this scenario. Frank was adamant that he would not return to the hospital or rehab. He wore a "do not resuscitate" bracelet, and on our refrigerator, I posted clear directives for everyone involved: "If something happens, do NOT call 911. We know this is going to be fatal; let's not make it worse than it is. *If I'm not here, CALL ME!*"

The medical system was harder to convince. At one point in 2019, Frank's doctor ordered an MRI, and I took him in for it. This is another moment, like getting dressed to go to the ER, that I now wonder about. Why did I do that? There was no point. Later that day, they called with the results—a blood clot in his carotid artery.

"You need to bring him in immediately," they urged.

"Why?" I asked. "What are you going to do?"

"Well, he needs to be here under observation."

"But what are you going to *do* for him?" I asked again.

"He needs to be under observation. He needs to be here immediately," they repeated.

"Well, we're home. If you need to observe him, you can come over. Although, we won't be home tonight, because we are going to a soccer game," I said.

"We don't think that's a good idea," they replied.

"Well, I don't think keeping Frank in the hospital, making him eat bad food and think about dying every minute, is a good idea when you can't *do* anything for him."

That was another one of those "Well, we never heard that one before" moments. We went to the soccer game that evening, which Frank thoroughly enjoyed.

On June 20, 2020, Frank went to see his neurologist, Dr. Machado, who had been treating Frank since his Parkinson's disease diagnosis in 2015. Frank came out of that appointment quite discouraged. I think his conversation with Dr. Machado made him realize he was going to continue having debilitating strokes, no matter what he did.

Frank had another stroke later that day. The strokes had eliminated his ability to feed himself. They had also rendered him unable to read, but Frank had read the paper every day for the last sixty years, and he still wanted it placed in his lap every day, even if he couldn't read it.

With each stroke, Frank's health deteriorated, and finally, one day, he told Dwayne that he'd had enough, that he was done. After Dwayne shared that with me, I crawled into the "hugging chair" with Frank. The hugging chair was his recliner, which we could both fit in. When Frank was feeling down, I would climb in the hugging chair and hug him.

"Dwayne told me you've had enough," I said. "We've climbed some big mountains together, and we're going to climb this one together too. You're not going to leave me out of this. I will do whatever you want, but I'm going to be right there with you."

I could feel the tears running down Frank's face as I pressed my cheek against his.

I pulled back to look at him. "Do you want to talk about it?" I asked.

"No," he whispered.

"Do you want me to talk about it?"

"Yes."

I pressed my cheek back against his. "I'm going to be with you every minute of every day, and you just make sure that you make clear anything you want."

That was the day Frank stopped eating. Two weeks later, as I lay beside him in the bed, my arms wrapped tightly around him for what would be the last time, I whispered in his ear, "I love you to the moon and back."

Frank exhaled a long "Ahhhhhh," and the love of my life was gone.

When I called Dwayne into the room, he looked at me and softly said, "I think he was just waiting to hear you say it."

Chapter 15

Connecting the Dots

When I mustered the courage to attend the annual Hartford Public Library gala in the fall of 2021, Frank had been gone for over a year, and I was still trying to navigate the next chapters of my life. I had been making slow progress.

A few months after Frank died, I received a call asking if I would be interested in joining a board. I thought, *Well, that's a surprise—that at seventy years old, I'm being asked to be on a board.* Then I thought of all the old men sitting on boards and thought, *Why shouldn't I, at seventy years old, be asked to be on a board?*

Their next question was, "Do you have the time?"

That was a bit of a magical moment for me because I suddenly realized that yes, I did, for the first time in my adult life, have all kinds of time. While Frank was ill, the only outside commitment I had maintained was chairing the CRDA. While that continued to be a big responsibility, it was all done within that six-block radius of our home, and with Leroy and then Dwayne as full-time caregivers, I had the freedom to come and go as needed. When COVID-19 hit, all our meetings were moved to Zoom, making the role even easier to manage. Outside of that, all my time had been spent with Frank, with occasional visits to Littleton to see my dad.

"I do have time," I said. "Please tell me more."

The board turned out to be for a NYSE company that did digitalized marketing, and the majority of the board members, including the chair, were women. They wanted me for the compensation committee, which was funny, because that's not a skill set I've ever claimed to have. By this stage in my career, however, I had thankfully learned to listen to what others believed I could do, even if I didn't see it myself.

How different my career would have been if I hadn't listened to the president of the bank when he encouraged me to leverage people's underestimation of me to my advantage; or to Bill Russell who believed I could run my own company; or to Rachel, Frank, and the TIAA-CREF shareholders who believed I could chair the Furr's/Bishop Inc. board of directors; or to Mike Tankersley who always believed not only in my capabilities but my ability to do the right thing; or to all the women in the Good Ol' Girls' Clubs (GOGCs) I brought together over the years (more on that in a moment).

So, when I was asked at seventy years old to serve on a board, even though I wasn't sure my skill set matched the role, I said, "Yes."

Once I was voted onto the board, I asked them, "Why did you want me? I don't have the industry experience; the company is in Los Angeles, and I'm on the East Coast. And," I added, "I'm seventy years old." Their response was that they wanted someone who was highly experienced; they knew I had served in a variety of industry settings, so the fact that I hadn't served in their industry was irrelevant to them. Finally, that I had experience with proxy contests was especially important to them because they were having shareholder challenges. I ticked all the boxes for experience in challenging environments.

The timing of my joining was perfect for the challenges the unexpected solicitations to buy their company created. Selling wasn't the intent when I was first approached, but shortly after I came on board, and completely unrelated to that fact, the company began receiving solicitations from companies who wanted to buy it. Selling a company with shareholders requires a specific set of procedures. If you do not represent the shareholders well or if they simply *think* you're not representing them well—such as selling the company for less than its value or them even thinking that you are—it opens the door for lawsuits. I ended up being highly beneficial to the shareholders, but in an unanticipated way.

Ultimately, the sale went to a private company, and so the board was disbanded within six months of my arrival. I would have liked a longer time with the women of that board. They offered a wide diversity of talents, the meetings were well run, and everyone was focused on adding value rather than the one-upmanship that occurs far too frequently on high-level, male-dominated boards. It was truly a pleasure to be part of this professional and talented group of women, and it provided me with an opportunity to reflect on my collective experience on boards.

With very few exceptions, I have always been the only woman on the board. And so often, it felt like my voice would simply go into the wind. Worse, there were moments where, after a pertinent question or valuable insight or idea I offered had been ignored, one of the men would repeat what I had just said, and it would be hailed as brilliant. It would have been exhausting to constantly point out that I'd said the exact same thing just moments ago—energy spent that I knew would not have changed the circumstances. My goal has always been to get the job done well. If that meant being quiet while others took credit for my work or, on occasion, sharing my idea with an individual and asking *him* to share it with the board so it would be taken seriously, so be it. As I listen to women my age talk about becoming invisible as we get older, I realize, as the only woman in the room, I've *always* been invisible!

Numbers don't lie. Rosabeth Moss Kanter's groundbreaking research introduced the concept of tokenism, showing how small numbers of underrepresented individuals face challenges in influencing decision-making.[11] Her work laid the foundation for understanding critical mass—the point at which representation becomes meaningful enough to drive change. It's the transition from being seen as token representatives to influential and integral contributors. When it comes to women in boardrooms, this theory has been repeatedly validated:

- Vicki W. Kramer, Alison M. Konrad, and Sumru Erkut found that boards with three or more women engage in more robust discussions, fostering better decision-making and collective intelligence.[12]
- Catalyst linked having three or more women on boards to improved governance and financial performance.[13]
- McKinsey & Company found that boards with at least three women exhibit stronger leadership behaviors in areas such as collaboration, strategic oversight, and innovation.[14]

11 Rosabeth Moss Kanter, *Men and Women of the Corporation* (Basic Books, 1977).

12 Vicki W. Kramer et al., *Critical Mass on Corporate Boards: Why Three or More Women Enhance Governance* (Wellesley Centers for Women, 2006).

13 "Quick Take: Why Diversity and Inclusion Matter," *Catalyst*, June 2024, https://www.catalyst.org/insights/2020/why-diversity-and-inclusion-matter.

14 "Women at the Top of Corporations: Making It Happen," *McKinsey & Company*, October 1, 2010, https://www.mckinsey.com/capabilities/people-and-organizational-performance/our-insights/women-at-the-top-of-corporations-making-it-happen.

Women were absent from these boards not from a lack of capable candidates but because male-dominated boards refused to acknowledge women's value. The GOGCs kept me from feeling stranded on a desert island.

The first GOGC I started was at Aetna. Glenda Reed—a woman of color—and I were the only women in a $33 billion investment division of three hundred people. Glenda was an amazing mentor, who guided me and shared such advice as: 1) If you're attending a department party, arrive early and leave early, because in order to work with people, you have to respect them, and you can't unsee what you see after an evening of drinking and partying; and 2) Stay away from watercooler discussions—they'll talk about you as soon as you leave. After I left Aetna, Glenda and I remained good friends, and when she passed, her daughter told me that Glenda wanted me to speak at her funeral. Glenda and her family were revered in Hartford, and four hundred people—including all of Hartford's community leaders—attended her funeral. My eulogy was preceded by a gospel minister; Glenda reached up from the grave to give me the stamp of approval in her community. That's who she was.

Barbara Durepo was the first female colleague beyond Glenda whom I connected with. She was the highest-ranking woman in bond investment and served as another member of the GOGC and as a mentor. When I discovered some other women who, like Barbara, Glenda, and me, held high-ranking positions that were typically only held by men, I reached out to them and suggested we all get together for lunch. There were six of us in total, and that first lunch was so incredibly helpful and productive for all of us that it became a monthly meeting of the GOGC.

Having this group of women to share stories with—stories that confirmed we were not all crazy and that the blatant aggressions were in fact real and happening to all of us—was critically important. In this group of women, we could openly discuss the two sets of rules that existed in corporate America and the power that the second set of rules held over our jobs and careers. Through our conversations, we discovered that there was a person in Aetna's hierarchy who had begun to question why women never seemed to get ahead at Aetna and why so many competent women were choosing to leave the organization. As you now know, three years after I left Aetna, its house of misogyny began to crumble.

When I began building The Hopgood Group, I joined the International Society of Hotel Consultants (ISHC). There, I found another small but amazing group of women. While we were not an official GOGC, we supported and cheered each other on every step of the way. It was at the ISHC that I met Rachel Roginsky, who would emphatically tell me that I *had* to accept the role of chair and CEO for Furr's and then proceeded to manage my business for a year to make that possible—simply incredible. All the women in this group were thrilled for me and absolutely loved the message it sent that a woman would chair a NYSE company. When one of us reached a new height, it lifted us all up.

My next experience with a GOGC, as I shared with you in chapter 10, came at the behest of the CEO of the NHC. Never in my days at Aetna could I have imagined that, at some future date, a male CEO would, in his efforts to elevate women into leadership positions, ask me to spearhead a GOGC. It was progress that I was proud to be part of.

The progress that continues to be made (albeit not enough of it) was evident in my founding of the GOGC within the CRDA. In my almost thirty years of board experience, the CRDA was the first board that had more than two female members. In thirty years! When the governor appointed me to chair the CRDA board in 2012, there were five women out of twelve board members (legislature hadn't made the thirteenth appointment yet).

The five of us would go to lunch regularly, as an informal GOGC. After one of these lunches, the governor saw me at a party and said, "I hear you've put together a women's group."

"I have."

"Quorum?" he asked.

"Women?" I responded, suggesting that women would *never* have the numbers for a quorum.

He laughed.

State-funded agencies such as the CRDA require a day's notice for any meeting of the board. Even if the meeting is not intended as a board meeting, if the equivalent of a quorum is present, it legally constitutes a board meeting.

The men on the board kept telling us they were going to start having lunch together, to which I would reply, "You can't. You constitute a quorum. You'd have to advertise your meeting and invite the public! Too bad."

It was a great group of women, and we invited in other women leaders. Our time together was incredibly valuable and allowed us to establish strong relationships we would not have otherwise made. That it drove our male counterparts crazy because they knew they were missing out was a bonus (and I was always certain to mention at our board meetings that the women would be having lunch together again ...).

When I reflect a bit further, I realize that, although we were not colleagues who lunched together, my true first GOGC comprised my mom and my aunts. How they interacted, supported, and believed in each other provided me with a front-row seat to the power of women both individually and collectively.

I was also well-versed in the power of the women who raised my dad. When my dad was only a month old, his father died. The men in his family were all gone before the Great Depression hit, and the women in his family—my grandmother, great-grandmother, and aunts—all banded together. They all moved so that they lived in the same apartment building in the Bronx. My great-grandmother babysat her grandchildren while my grandmother, her sisters, and her aunts went off to work. The women in my family, on both sides, have been nothing short of powerhouses. Powerhouses who chose husbands who respected and supported them.

Outside of my childhood bubble, society was constantly reinforcing the idea that women were not capable, so growing up in the environment my parents raised me in was powerful stuff—so powerful that I was not fully aware of society's warped concept of what a women's role should be until the fall of 1967, when one of my male professors at Northeastern asked all the "girls" to move to the front, so that "those of us who want to learn will have the ability to learn." As you read in chapter 3, all thirty-three of us did as we were told.

That was the only time I simply stood up and moved to the front "so the men could learn."

Over the years, I have taken every opportunity at conferences to speak about the men who did not support me—the men who were no-shows when I needed them to step up. Stories like my boss who knocked on my door late one night to tell me he was lonely, and the boss who thrived on constantly degrading my work and value, and the insurance guy on the homebuilder's board who sexually harassed me for months until the other men on the board stepped up.

"This," I tell them, "was the first time in my career that any man had stepped up on my behalf when I was being harassed. I bring this up because stepping up as a man will make a difference in a woman's life. You need to pay attention, and if you see a man harassing, degrading, or disrespecting a woman, you need to step up."

These audiences often comprised mostly men, and I like to think I made an impact. At one conference in 2017, one of the men on the panel was in tears when I finished my story. He was a colleague who knew me well, but he had not known the harassment and disrespect I had endured over the years. When I saw how emotional he was, my first thought was, *Oh my goodness. I didn't mean to do that,* but maybe that's exactly what we should mean to do: insist on the awareness and accountability necessary for change.

Chapter 16

Leaving a Legacy

I pride myself on knowing when it's time for me to go, and I knew in November 2022 that it was time for me to leave the bubble of sadness that Hartford had become. It was a bittersweet transition that was three years in the making.

In 2019, about a year after Frank's first stroke, Kathy sat me down and said, "Suzanne, it's time for you to start planning your next life so that when Frank dies, you don't fall off the cliff."

It was painful to even consider what a "next life" that would be mine and mine alone would look like, but Kathy was right, and I'm grateful for her courage in telling me to take this early step. Within a couple of months of our conversation, I bought a multifamily house in Littleton, New Hampshire, and began renovations to split one of the units to create a one-bedroom apartment. I would eventually move into this apartment in the fall of 2022, and it remains my primary residence.

This time provided me with the space to appreciate and say goodbye to the community that Frank and I had contributed to over our almost forty years together—a community that we cherished and were incredibly grateful for. Simply residing in a community was never enough for

Frank and me, and we had both immersed ourselves in Hartford and contributed to the well-being of the community we chose to live in.

Frank, as I've shared, committed his time and talents to the Mark Twain House for many years. But prior to the Mark Twain House and Frank's retirement in 2002, he had begun what would be his Hartford legacy, serving on the board of another organization near and dear to his heart: the Bushnell Park Conservancy (formerly the Bushnell Park Foundation). When we stepped out of our condo building, we were just a few feet from the park. It was in Bushnell Park that two hundred of us gathered in 2020 for Frank's memorial service, in honor of the man and his legacy. Over a span of time between 1997 and 2020, Frank also served on the boards of Hands On Hartford, the Greater Hartford Transit District, the City of Hartford Pension Commission, the Citizens Network of the Capital Region, the Hartford Business Improvement District, and the Consortium of Neighborhood Leaders. He was also the first president of our neighborhood association, South Downtown.

Frank was retired for almost twenty years, during which he could have spent his time serving only his own needs, but that is not the man Frank was. In everything he did, Frank thought of the impact on others and how he might contribute to the lives of the people around him. So, while Leroy and Dwayne were always taken aback by how many people stopped to say hello to Frank, whether they were wheeling him through the park, at the gym, or simply out and about in Hartford, it never came as a surprise to me. Frank was a genuine human being whom people naturally gravitated to.

My first foray into the Hartford community was in the '80s when Bill Russell recommended me for the Hartford Downtown Council. I did my best to lend my voice to the council as a city dweller, but it was often hard to be heard over the wealthy suburbanites (mostly men) who thought they knew better about what was best for the city.

This is where I learned that if I wanted any of my ideas to reach the discussion stage, they needed to be presented by one of the men.

A decade later, while I was busy building The Hopgood Group, I was invited to participate in a two-year leadership course sponsored by the American Leadership Forum and based in Hartford. The purpose of the course was to gather a diverse group of influential people who, if united, had the potential to improve the community of Hartford. The group comprised African American, Latino, and White men and women who worked within nonprofit and for-profit organizations, as well as for government agencies. We engaged in wide-ranging discussions on leadership and community alongside trust-building exercises. The course culminated in an Outward Bound experience, climbing Galena Mountain in Colorado.

At the start of the course, we drew names for partners. My partner would be the Hartford police chief who, I learned, carried nitroglycerin pills with him. Anxious to determine his fitness long before our trip to the top of Galena Mountain, I suggested we start biking four mornings a week. If there was going to be an issue, I thought it best it happen there in Hartford, where any call for help for the chief would likely receive a quicker response than from the top of Galena Mountain.

So began our six o'clock in the morning bike rides. On our first morning out, the chief and I were joined by another member of the group, Richard Weaver-Bey (Glenda Reed's cousin). Richard was an incredible biker, and he knew how to map out a safe bike route in and around the city. The three of us began riding from six o'clock to a quarter past seven, four mornings a week. As time went on, the other members of the group joined in, and we became a different kind of team.

We had few rules: Wear a helmet, we leave at six o'clock sharp, alert the person in front of you if you or a car will be passing them, and finally, everyone's responsible for the person behind them. That last rule meant you needed to pay attention if the person behind you ran into trouble, whether that was because of a fall, flat tire, or broken chain—if they stopped, you needed to stop and help and alert the person in front of you to the situation.

As you can imagine, over the next two years, we became a very close-knit group. Those morning bike rides were wonderful, and we joked that during our time together talking and biking, we were able to solve all the city's problems (and, occasionally, someone had to remind us that the goal was *biking*, not just talking). Our summer rides were longer and sometimes took us to Frank's and my home in Old Saybrook (forty-five miles away). One trip took us forty miles north, to Retired Colonel Ron Copes's house (Ron was Glenda Reed's brother, who joined our bike group when we were in our second year), where his family prepared a breakfast suitable for a hundred-mile bike ride.

What I learned most through the leadership course and our bike rides was to hone my listening skills to really hear what people were saying. At one of our initial meetings, we were outdoors, and Richard expressed his discomfort with all the mosquitoes flying around us. While he attempted to swat the pests away, he said, "This is really bothering me." Even if he hadn't said anything, his body language said it all.

Finally, by the third time Richard clearly stated his discomfort, I said, "Why don't we go inside?" We did, and I thought, *We have a leader here who's teaching us leadership skills, but he's not listening to a team member who is clearly making his needs known.* The solution was so simple, but the leader wasn't paying attention—that stuck with me.

Listening is also about asking questions—and really taking in the answer—to expand your knowledge base and your awareness of the world around you. I remember on one morning ride, I was riding with Richard and Ron through a wealthy and White neighborhood in West Hartford when Ron said to Richard, "If it was just the two of us, we would not be biking here."

"No, we wouldn't," agreed Richard.

This led to a whole discussion on why neither of these gentlemen would ever leave their house unless they were in a suit or their bike-riding attire, and even then, they moved with caution.

These were things that I, a North Country, New Hampshire, White girl had no idea about. Growing up, my parents had employed both White and Black people, so it wasn't that I hadn't been exposed to other races, but just as I had been unaware of sexism growing up, I had honestly been equally unaware of racism because my parents and aunts had treated everyone with equal respect. The kitchen at my parents' summer resort was run by Chef Jasper and Baker Dorothy—both African American. It was made very clear to all of us that the kitchen was their domain, and we were all to do as they instructed, no questions asked. In my immediate world, I simply never perceived any difference between how women and men were treated or how Black and White people were treated.

I became very good at asking Richard, Ron, and Glenda what I thought were stupid questions, and I am incredibly grateful for their patience in providing me the space to ask those questions and to have them answered. Their answers expanded my awareness of and perspective on living in a city that primarily comprised minorities who were surrounded by affluent White communities, an awareness and perspective that would inform my later work as chair of the CRDA.

By the time our leadership group embarked on its final mission of climbing Galena Mountain, our trust and deep respect for each other was solid, and our climb, though incredibly mentally and physically challenging, was a resounding success (and no, thankfully, the chief had no need for his nitroglycerin pills that day or on any of our bike rides). When we returned from that trip, I thought our morning bike riding group would come to an end. But instead, everyone wanted to stick with it and expand it to include whoever wanted to join. Today, some thirty years later, the riders have changed, but the group I began for the purpose of ensuring the health and safety of my leadership partner is still biking through the streets of Hartford in the wee hours of the morning—an unwitting legacy I am proud to have created.

As it turned out, listening and asking more (and sometimes stupid) questions was the perfect recipe for a successful workout person. My persistence in digging away at problems, combined with my willingness to ask the questions others avoided, led to my sought-after expertise in uncovering the truth—truth that would lead to solutions that weren't always popular but were right for the situation (I promise, Mike!).

My need to dig for the truth is what set my role with the CRDA in motion. At some point in 2011, I discovered that the management company at my homeowner's association (HOA) was effectively stealing money, and I began to discreetly get to the bottom of it. I learned a long time ago how to ask questions that get you answers without showing your hand right out of the gate. You ask for information bit by bit. Rather than asking for the financials, I asked to see the waste management bills for the last five years. Then I asked for the water bills, and then, in good time, I asked for the heating bills. As I was collecting this seemingly innocuous information, I was building a spreadsheet of our HOA's five-year financial history.

In the end, the Connecticut Department of Consumer Protection would outlaw this management company from ever managing our HOA again and, to protect us, it would establish a set of other rules the condo association had to abide by.

As discreet as I thought I'd been in my information gathering, another condo owner in the building, unbeknownst to me, had watched me build and eventually close my case. He served as the governor's general counsel, and we'd become friends.

After the HOA case closed in late 2011, this individual called and took me by surprise when he said, "The governor is setting up the board of the CRDA, and he wants to appoint you to it."

"OK ..."

"He wants you to be chair," he added.

Huh, I thought. *The governor and his legal counsel think I should chair the CRDA. I think I'll listen.* (As if Frank would have ever let me turn that one down.)

I would subsequently learn that I was a top pick because the governor knew that some of the personalities going on the board would require some pushback, and he was confident I would be willing and able to provide that pushback (i.e., badassery) when necessary.

The governor made sure that we had a board that consisted of an impressive group of corporate executives, mayors, and Connecticut commissioners who could get things done, and he was tremendously supportive of the work we did. Though, as I shared in chapter 13, the CRDA board did have a moment of upheaval between the board members, it was a moment we were able to work through and resolve together.

Over the ten years I served on the board, we worked cohesively for the betterment of our beautiful community of Hartford. In addition to the newly created three thousand housing units, we initiated the long process of renovating the XL Center and the state-owned Rentschler Field.

Frank and I committed our hearts and souls to our community in Hartford, and that community of support flowed back to us tenfold when Frank was dying and through my transition to the next chapter in my life. That support continues today. In its fundraising efforts, our NPR station has begun associating a person in town with its GivingTuesday matching grants. On GivingTuesday in 2023, the donations for the matching grant I had offered shot from $50,000 to $95,000 when the station aired the recording of me talking about Frank and his legacy of giving in Hartford. It was an incredibly emotional and proud moment for me.

Hartford will forever be *our* home, and I continue to rent a studio apartment in the city for my frequent visits. But today, *my* home sits squarely in Littleton, New Hampshire—and yes, I have already been busy uncovering truths and creating a new GOGC!

Conclusion

And Suddenly, I'm Seventy-Five

Returning to the familiarity of my childhood home of Littleton certainly made my emotional transition out of Hartford a bit easier. I had continued to spend time in Littleton over the years, visiting my dad. My mom passed away in 2002 after succumbing to complications from Alzheimer's disease, but my dad was still with us until July 2022, when he passed at the age of 101 from, according to his death certificate, "extreme old age." He was sharp and active to the end—we even played golf on his 101st birthday! So, I had maintained many connections here, and because of Mom and Dad's commitment to the betterment of Littleton, my maiden name, McAvoy, still carries enormous weight. Just as I continue to honor Frank's legacy in Hartford, I'm dedicating performances and granite benches in honor of my parents' legacy in Littleton.

I have also been busy making new friends and discovering new ways to offer my assistance to the Littleton community. When someone suggested I offer aid to one of the organizations in town, the role they were looking for me to fill wasn't something I had done before, but I continue to be open to trying new things and finding new ways to help, so I said yes. After doing a bit of work, I discovered something that didn't seem quite right to me, and so, as I often do, I began to dig for the truth. I began by asking those seemingly innocuous and stupid questions, and what I found was a sticky, unsettling mess. Normally, this type of workout (even as a volunteer in retirement, I was still finding myself in these workout situations) is my wheelhouse, and I jump right in. But in this moment of my life, I had to sit back and remind myself that I am, at seventy-five, an old lady (I have come to enjoy the leverage that throwing around the phrase "I'm an old lady" wields me—there is power in old age) and that I had returned to my hometown to take care of myself.

So, when I saw how deep this potential workout would run, I handed it off to another capable person and committed myself to continuing to help in ways that connected me more deeply to the individuals in our community. I have been a listening ear and source of support to friends who have recently lost their partners, and I have become involved in my church (something of a surprise and delight to my friends) because it is filled with people who are trying to help other people, and that's the niche I want to be in. I naturally landed in our church's kitchen, helping to serve our weekly free community meals. When I saw how loose the guidelines for working in the kitchen were, I had to establish rules appropriate for a communal kitchen. "If you don't need to be in the kitchen, stay out," I pronounced that first evening—which made everyone burst out laughing, but they do mostly listen.

I have been profoundly touched by the people I meet at these community meals, and I love being a part of this wonderful team of community-minded people who get good things done. Through the holiday season, every time I'm out and about in town, I bring bags of goodies to drop off and say "Thank you, I appreciate you" to the people who keep our little community running. These are the seemingly small but incredibly important things I did not have the time to do when I was working and serving on community and corporate boards.

Now, with more time, I'm also committed to traveling all over the world. My now-solo adventures were one of the more difficult transitions into the next chapters of my life. Just as I had come to realize that Frank had been the one who orchestrated our social life, I had to come to terms with the fact that, as a woman traveling alone, I was not the confident traveler I had thought myself to be. My confidence and eagerness to jump on planes that would take us all over the world existed because Frank was such an amazing and eager navigator. Planning well-organized and incredibly well-researched trips is a skill I am purposely developing.

My first trip back to Thailand without Frank was made easier by my willing traveling companions: my niece, Cheryl McAfee, and my good friends Jennifer and Stephanie. Jennifer and Stephanie are avid cyclists like me. My niece is a serious hiker, so she's in great shape, but she's not a cyclist. I recommended she go on some rides in advance of the trip so her butt would build the necessary calluses to survive a week of daily bike rides. After her first ride, she understood what I meant and prepared accordingly.

We made that trip in January 2023, and it was amazing. Showing Cheryl, Stephanie, and Jennifer Thailand through Frank's eyes was the perfect perspective for my first trip back. We spread some of Frank's ashes on the beach of our favorite resort. I ventured back to Thailand alone in January 2025—not to bike this time but to spend extended time in Chiang Mai, where Frank and I had only spent a couple of nights at a time. A friend of a friend, a US citizen, has lived there for eighteen years, and he took me under his wing. This trip, I experienced Thailand in a way that Frank and I did not. And I've rented an apartment in Chiang Mai so I can spend time there whenever I wish, especially when it's negative ten degrees in Littleton.

In between these two trips to Thailand, I traveled with a tour group to Japan. Japan is a country of rules, and so I figured I couldn't get into too much trouble on my own. One of the women I met on the trip had recently had hip surgery and walked with two poles. I offered her my assistance on our various walking tours, and at one point, she turned to me and said, "You are the nicest person I have ever met."

I burst out laughing. "No one has ever said that to me." I couldn't wait to tell my friends back home, and, sure enough, they laughed as hard as I had.

Now, on that same trip, another traveler told me I was the most obnoxious person she had ever met. My first thought was, *I can do obnoxious if you want,* but my now-wise, old-lady self said, "Thank you for sharing that."

I was proud of myself for not, as my niece would say, engaging with crazy. I don't think I would have been able to respond in that way even five years ago. My friends also found this experience quite amusing. And the new friends I made on the trip took every opportunity to say, "Isn't Suzanne just the nicest person?" whenever the woman who called me obnoxious was in earshot—I couldn't have orchestrated a more hilarious scenario. Little did she know how much laughter her unkind comment would provide us—laughter remains as necessary for me as oxygen.

I remember shortly after Frank died, Mike Tankersley said to me, "In all the years I've known you, you have had an incredible ability to break the tension in any meeting by making people laugh—even when there is absolutely nothing funny about the situation."

"Really?" I asked. Even now, I keep learning new things about myself.

"Yes. And," he continued, "I think you have a minimum daily requirement for laughing. And my guess is it's like 142 times a day. After Frank died, you dropped below your minimum daily requirement."

That made me laugh, and it also made me realize that I was now dependent on myself to meet my daily laughter requirement, which I continue to build back up one laugh at a time.

When I returned from Japan, I visited my pastor and shared with her how stunned I was that someone had said I was the nicest person they had ever met.

"Well," she said, "my guess is your career did not lend itself to people telling you how nice you were."

She was right. My career required that I hold people accountable. And while accountability can and should be handled with respect, it rarely earns you a reputation for being nice.

Not that I mind. Being seen as nice has never been a priority for me. When I think about writing my obituary (yes, this is something I think about these days), I care that people remember that I showed up, that I fought for what mattered, that I made a difference, and that I left things better than I found them even if that did, and occasionally still does, require some ass-kicking.

Since my trip to Japan, my adventures have taken me through Andalusia, Spain, and the vibrant markets of Morocco. Egypt may be next on my horizon, and I'm already envisioning more time in my Chiang Mai apartment. Throughout these journeys—and, indeed, throughout my entire career—I've discovered that making people laugh creates connection, eases tension, and brings joy to everyone involved. It's a skill I've honed over the years, and one that serves me well in retirement just as it did in boardrooms. I hope I've brought you a few laughs along the way as you've read my story.

I am still a force. And nothing reminds me of that more than a lifetime of amazing women—the many members of GOGCs, which I continue to organize—who have shaped my life in ways I'm only just beginning to fully appreciate.

Unlike our earlier years navigating the male-dominated world of corporate America, the GOGCs no longer need these connections to survive. But we do need them to remember who we were before we retired—and, more importantly, to inspire each other as we decide who we want to be now. These fun, fierce, and formidable groups of women refuse to be invisible. And that, to me, is what truly matters.

www.ingramcontent.com/pod-product-compliance
Lightning Source LLC
LaVergne TN
LVHW050550120926
847757LV00002B/30
* 9 7 9 8 8 9 1 8 8 0 9 5 5 *